MARY BOUGHT A LITTLE LAMB
AND THIS IS HOW SHE COOKED IT

RHODA NATION was born into a farming family in Cambridge, New Zealand. She qualified as a nurse and spent four years overseas on nursing duties then returned to New Zealand to housekeep for her widowed father, who is still remembered with affection as having been Master of the Waikato Hunt for a record term of years.

In World War Two, during which she served as a Detachment Commandant of the Red Cross, she married and in 1945 settled with her husband and their first child on a Central Hawke's Bay sheep farm. Cooking for a growing family further extended her knowledge of the uses of mutton and lamb, and in the early 1960s she decided to record her knowledge of the subject in book form to stimulate interest in this branch of cookery.

In the years following, with the aid of interested friends, she conducted precise research into the formulation and practical testing of the recipes presented in this book.

She lived to enjoy the phenomenal success of the first edition of this book and to make the revisions incorporated in this edition.

MARY BOUGHT A LITTLE LAMB

AND THIS IS HOW SHE COOKED IT

by

RHODA NATION

BAILEY BROTHERS AND SWINFEN LTD.

Folkestone

Published in Great Britain by
Bailey Brothers & Swinfen Ltd.
1975

SBN 561 00221 5

Printed in Great Britain by
Clarke, Doble & Brendon Ltd, Plymouth

DEDICATION

For the underprivileged children to whose needs
Save the Children Fund
dedicates its work.

CONTENTS

FOREWORD

by LADY ORMOND

THE BOOK OF GENESIS tells us that Abel was a keeper of sheep, and throughout the ages Man has depended on this animal for food and clothing of the finest quality.

The economy of both Australia and New Zealand was founded on mutton and wool. But whereas wonderful advances have been made in the processing of wool into textiles, home cooks have been slow to explore and exploit the full potential of mutton and lamb. Yet these low-cost, high-protein meats can, under guidance, provide exciting, economical dishes.

Mrs Rhoda Nation, with her long experience of farming life and years of cookery research and experiment, has built into this book a wealth of new ideas—practical, simple, successful—on lamb and mutton cookery. Her recipes are within the everyday skills of the average home cook, and most of her recommended dishes are easy on the household budget.

The sales of this book will, by Mrs Nation's wish and through the medium of the Save the Children Fund, help the hungry children of the world. I commend it to all those who, while appreciating the pleasures and benefits of good cookery, remember those who are in need.

PREFACE

THE URGE to write this book goes back a long way. Kindled and cajoled by family, friends and women's organisations, I have, at long last, put together some of the results of my many experiments with lamb, hogget and mutton meats. I have given special attention to the less expensive cuts, and have also included favourite recipes from friends.

The main purpose of this book is to introduce to the novice an interesting and varied approach to this versatile culinary field, and its recipes will suit all purses and palates. For example, you will find new ideas for picnics, barbecues, quick lunches, winter family meals, and a delicious Christmas dinner. The general notes on the basic cooking, seasoning and compatibility of flavours will, I hope, encourage cooks to produce their own special creations.

A word of warning: first, become thoroughly acquainted with all the specific requirements. Introduce new flavours very gradually, and learn to substitute ingredients—if one is not in your cupboard, use something similar. (The chapter on the use of herbs and spices will help you here.) And don't be afraid of the cheaper cuts which require long, slow cooking. I have included a number of delicious recipes for these economical dishes which are well worth the effort required.

When planning a dinner include at least one, preferably two, colourful vegetables. When serving, place them in small quantities to add interest to the arrangement. Remember—garnishing is a split-second procedure which completes the appetising picture. Often the dinner-table is the only place where the family gathers together at one time, and the serving of a tasty well-cooked meal can be an important contribution to harmony in the home.

The subject of this book brings to mind our hungry children overseas. In sharing my royalty with the Save the Children Fund, I trust that a number of these children will benefit.

In conclusion I wish to thank my husband, family and many friends who have helped to make this publication possible, and the New Zealand Meat Producers' Board for their permission to reproduce the diagrams.

Rhoda Nation

Chapter 1

LAMB, HOGGET AND MUTTON

SPRING LAMB:
Aged from 12 to 18 weeks. Light pinkish meat, creamy mellow fat and very little bone.

LAMB (WEANED):
Aged 4½ to 9 months. There is a slight deepening in the colour of the flesh.

HOGGET:
Aged 9 to 20 months. Flesh a deeper pink, fat whiter and firmer than lamb.

YOUNG MUTTON
Aged 20 months to 2 years. Flesh pinky-red. Fat firm.

MATURE MUTTON:
Aged 2 to 5 years. Flesh deepens to red with age, fat is white and becomes brittle.

JOINTS

SCRAG END NECK: About fifty per cent bone. Section and use in stews, curries and casseroles. After long slow cooking it is nutritious and full of flavour.

MIDDLE NECK: (Chops behind shoulderblade). Has more meat and less bone. Lamb or hogget left whole and jointed or sold as Spanish Neck (the middle neck jointed with very short rib bones) are popular for roasting, braising, poaching or, with or without bone, sectioned, trimmed and crumbed as cutlets. Also sold as chops for a braise, casserole or stew. Requires long slow cooking.

BEST END NECK: (Centre or Rib Loin). Consists of six or seven cutlets in one piece, sometimes called a rack. As a roast the joint may be chined (backbone removed) to simplify carving. Have bones removed if it is to be stuffed and rolled. The lamb or hogget cutlets are perfect to grill or sauté for a quick meal.

LOIN: Thick, choice, fleshy joint with little bone, available in one piece or sold as large meaty chops. As a roast have it jointed, also boned and rolled as well unless it is to be stuffed. The chops have a short T-bone and are ideal to grill or sauté. Noisettes are cut to the required thickness from the boned and rolled loin. Saddle of lamb consists of the right and left loins before they have been split by the butcher. A roast for a special occasion.

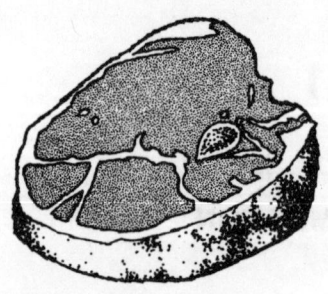

Chump Chop or Steak

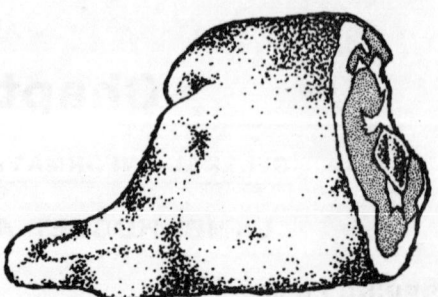

Whole Leg Roast

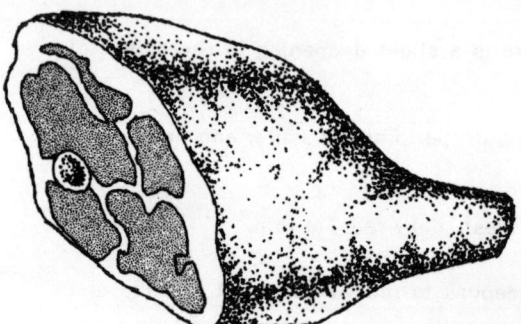

Half Leg Roast
(Shank end)

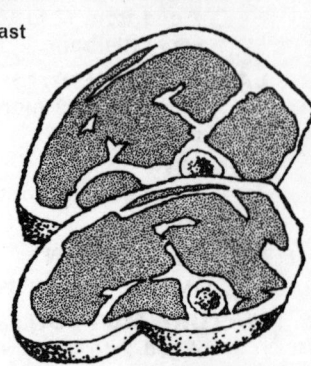

Leg Chops or
Tender Steak

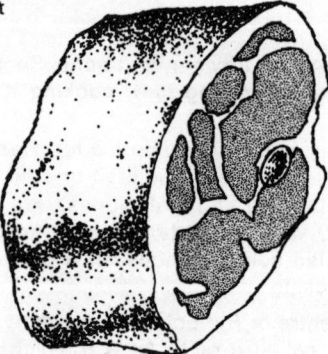

Fillet or Butt Leg Roast (steak)

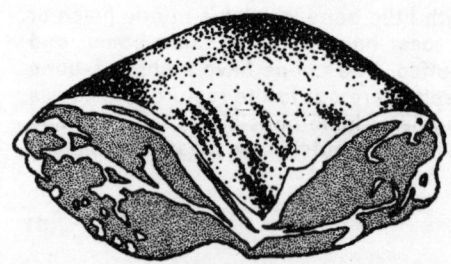

Square Cut Shoulder Roast

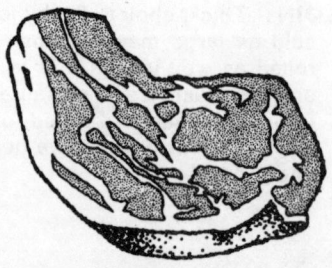

Blade Chop

USUAL CUTS

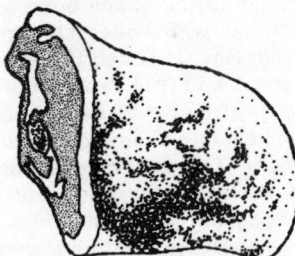

Loin Roast

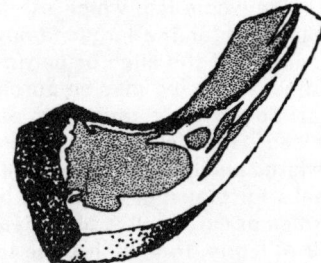

Rib or Centre Loin Chop (cutlet)

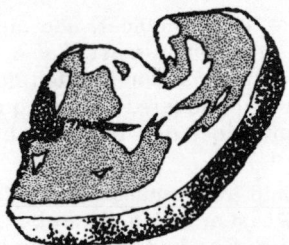

Loin Chop

Best End Neck or Rib (rack) Roast

Shanks

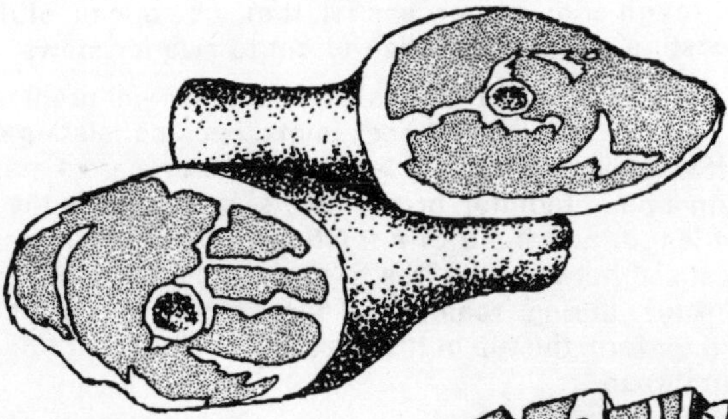

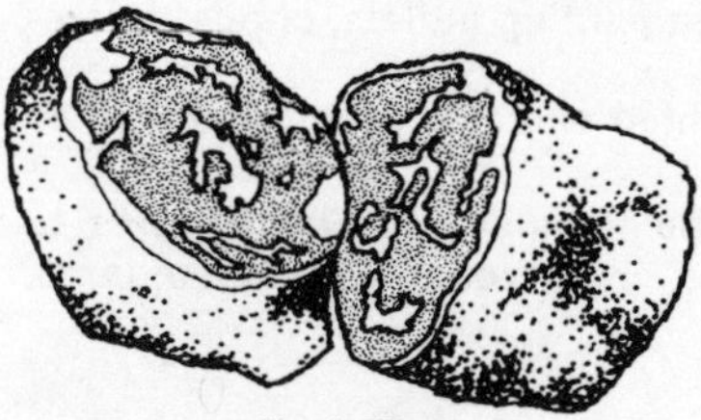

Neck Slices

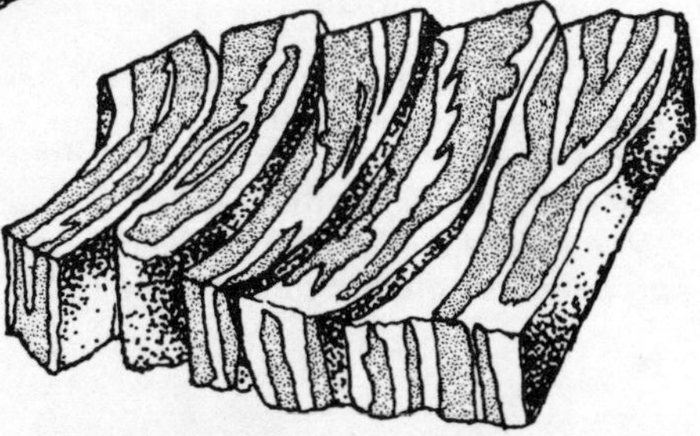

Riblets

LEG: The whole leg, which extends from the loin to the shank bone, is an ideal roast for the larger family. Roast or braise with bone. To simplify carving have the aitch or pelvic bone removed. Have it boned if it is to be stuffed. Half a leg may be purchased. The shank end (from shank bone to aitch bone) has a large proportion of lean meat and may be roasted or braised. The thick end of this joint may also be cut into chump chops which are large and meaty with a small amount of bone. The meat may be cut into steaks for braising, or cubed, diced or minced for lamburgers, pies, casseroles or curries. It is also ideal for oriental cooking. The fillet end or butt end of leg is from aitch bone to loin. Have it boned to stuff as a roast or slice across the grain into tender rump steaks. Excellent to grill or sauté. The shanks provide a tasty meal if braised or stewed. Spring lamb shanks may be grilled.

FOREQUARTER: A combination of middle neck, shoulder, and most of the breast. Neatly jointed it is a popular large family roast. For a small family, see Shoulder, Middle Neck and Breast. This joint is often divided into two joints only: square shoulder, which is squared below shoulder blade and includes rib bones, so is a thick joint. Joint ribs to roast or braise. Also Spanish Neck (see Middle Neck page 11).

SHOULDER: From the forequarter, a plump joint smaller than a leg. It consists of the knuckle end and the blade. Roast or braise. It may be boned and rolled as well, unless it is to be stuffed. The boned joint simplifies carving. With excess fat removed the meat may also be cut into steaks for a frying pan braise or casserole. Mince or chop finely for lamburgers, or cube for meat pies, curries, etc.

BREAST: Consists of ribs which, if jointed, make a delicious roast. Sectioned into riblets, lamb or hogget breast is succulent grilled or barbecued. Otherwise cut to size required for stews, casseroles, fricassees, curries, etc. Mature mutton requires long slow cooking.

FLAP: A continuation of the breast, usually five top rib ends extending to the flank. Trim rough ends and excess fat. It may be boned, stuffed and rolled for slow roasting in a covered dish or cut to size for stews, curries, etc.

CROWN: A succulent joint to roast. The butcher will prepare the crown. It is formed by a pair of best end neck joints, each consisting of six to seven cutlets, left whole and jointed. It is possible to prepare a more economical crown using a pair of jointed breast riblets. In each case the rib ends must be of even length and freed of a fraction of the surrounding tissue. This should be sliced between the ribs to an even depth (about $\frac{1}{4}$ inch) to allow even shrinkage during roasting. These meatless rib ends, protected while roasting, form the top of the crown. The circle is formed and secured with strong thread.

If requested, the butcher will use a saw when jointing cutlets, chops, a forequarter or square shoulder, etc.

Pre-packed or pre-cut meats are already jointed and may be offered with or without bone, and often stuffed.

When possible order in advance joints which require several minutes to prepare i.e. boned, or boned and rolled joints, crown roast or saddle of lamb.

AMOUNTS TO PURCHASE

1 lb meat without bone: 4 average servings i.e. steaks or boned joints, cubed, diced or minced meats and liver, brains and sweetbreads. For 1 average serving: 1 sheep's tongue, 1 sheep's heart, 2 lamb's tongues or 3 kidneys.

1 lb meat with a proportionately small amount of bone: 2½ average servings i.e. loin, leg or chump chops, leg joint or shank end leg.

1 lb meat with more bone than above: 2 average servings i.e. fillet end of leg, shoulder, cutlets, neck chops, flaps.

1 lb meat with a large amount of bone: 1½ average servings i.e. scrag end neck, breast and shanks.

FREEZING, COOKING AND THAWING OF MEAT

Home-killed meat should be hung (overnight if possible) before preparing it for the freezer, otherwise it will be less palatable when cooked like freshly killed meat. Meat cuts should be wiped clean with a damp cloth if necessary and jointed before packaging. They should be wrapped in moisture-vapour proof wrapping, excluding as much air as possible.

Suggested maximum storage period at 0° F for lamb, hogget and mutton is 8 to 12 months.

For precooked meat i.e. Stews, etc   3 to 6 months.
                                Pies   2 to 4 months.

To cook frozen cuts allow approximately 1½ times normal cooking time i.e. from fresh state 20 mins per lb; from frozen state 30 mins per lb.

Thaw frozen meat at room temperature or in refrigerator if time permits. Leave meat in freezer wrapping until thawed, to retain as much juice as possible.

Thawing: 24 hrs in refrigerator for roast; 4-5 hrs for chops, etc.

MEASUREMENTS

Unless specifically stated, all measurements used in this book are level.

The cup used is an 8 oz breakfast cup.

The only way to achieve accuracy when measuring ingredients is to purchase a standard set of measuring spoons and a reliable set of kitchen scales.

Note: Warm the spoon when using it to measure butter, fat, honey or golden syrup.

ROASTS, POT ROASTS AND BRAISES

To Roast
> To bake in an uncovered shallow pan with or without fat or oil, in an oven. This cooking term is used in the general sense i.e. to cook, usually in an oven.

To Pot-roast
> The joint is placed in a pan with a firm lid and baked with or without stock, either in the oven, over a heated element, or in an electric frying pan.

To Braise
> Joint is first seared (page 134) or browned in hot cooking oil or fat before the stock is added. It is then baked in a firmly-covered casserole or baking dish, or simmered over bottom heat in a heavy based sauce-pan covered with a close-fitting lid, or in an electric frying pan.

Any portion of a lamb, hogget or young mutton carcase will roast successfully. The less expensive cuts (which may be tenderised in a marinade, see Chapter 18), if well seasoned and pot-roasted in a covered pan will produce a delicious joint.

To Season Joints: The tendency is to add insufficient salt to sheepmeats. Allow 1 teaspoon of salt for 1 lb of meat plus ½ teaspoon for each subsequent 1 lb. Before cooking, rub salt thoroughly (a frozen joint excepted) into the joint. It will be completely absorbed and the flavour enriched. Sprinkle it generously with freshly-ground pepper or finely crushed peppercorns. If roasting a frozen joint, remove it from the oven when thawed (halfway through the cooking period) and sprinkle with the salt and pepper.

A Meat Thermometer (abbreviation MT). The advantages of this reasonably priced instrument are not as well known as they should be. Meat is an expensive necessity and this thermometer, which is very simple to use, gives the assurance that roast and braised joints will be cooked to perfection. Undercooking, overcooking, unnecessary shrinkage and drying out are avoided. After seasoning the joint, insert the thermometer into the thickest part where the bulb must rest and **not** be in contact with bone. When the thermometer reaches the given reading set out in the timetable opposite, the meat is cooked. If roasting a frozen joint, insert the thermometer when applying the seasoning, halfway through the cooking period.

General Method of Roasting a Joint
Sprinkle 2 tablespoons of flour in roasting pan to form a rich brown gravy base. Add joint (fat side uppermost). Basting is required only when a glaze or marinade is used. If vegetables are to be roasting around a lean joint and the pan is large, add 2-4 tablespoons of fat.
A shank end of leg which has little outside fat should be turned several times while roasting. Alternatively place this joint on a low rack in the pan and give it one turn halfway through the cooking period. When using a rack, remember to increase the cooking period at least 10 minutes per lb. Before placing a roast in a pan to be covered, sprinkle in 1-2 tablespoons of flour. As steam from the joint, or the stock, aids the cooking of a covered roast, follow the shorter cooking period set out in the timetable opposite. Mature mutton joints, which may first be marinated, are the exception as they always require a long slow cooking period.

To Dish a Joint: To avoid fat drippings on a serving dish from the joint or roasted vegetables, place a wire rack on a fireproof plate and lift joint and vegetables on to this. Keep warm while preparing gravy. Immediately before serving, slip joint on to heated serving dish and arrange vegetables round it. All hot meats should be served piping hot on hot plates.

To Pot-roast in Frying pan: Season meat as for oven cooking (p. 134). Heat frying pan 300°. Place meat in pan fat side up. Replace lid with vent closed. Halfway through cooking time turn roast to brown other side. Roast vegetables around meat, turning frequently, with vent open. If necessary crisp under grill. Allow 1 lb joint 30 to 45 minutes and each subsequent 1 lb 20 to 35 minutes depending upon age and thickness of joint.

This timetable for roasting sheepmeats is given as a general guide. Such factors as size and shape of joint, the amount of fat present, and the variation in stove temperatures, prevent complete accuracy. Oven temperature equivalents are approximate. Consult the charts supplied with your cooker, or obtain one from the manufacturer of your particular model.

Electric and Gas Oven Equivalents

200°F	Regulo ½	350°F	Regulo 4	450°F	Regulo 8
250°F	Regulo 1	375°F	Regulo 5	475°F	Regulo 9
300°F	Regulo 2	400°F	Regulo 6	500°F	Regulo 10
325°F	Regulo 3	425°F	Regulo 7		

	Oven temperature	Minutes per lb	Thermometer reading internal temperature
Lamb	350°F Regulo 4	25 to 30	180°
Spring Lamb (covered)	325°F Regulo 3	20 to 25	180°
Hogget	350°F Regulo 4	30 to 35	182°
Young Mutton	325°F Regulo 3	35 to 40	185°
Mature Mutton	325°F Regulo 3	40 to 45	185°
Mature Mutton	250°F Regulo 1	45 to 50	185°
Mature Mutton (covered)	250°-300°F Regulo 1-2	45 to 50	185°

For a small roast up to 3½ lbs allow the longer cooking period.

For a large roast allow the shorter cooking period.

Allow: A rolled roast an extra 5 to 10 minutes per lb.

A joint straight from a refrigerator and under 5 lbs an extra 5 minutes per lb.

A larger joint from a refrigerator an extra 10 minutes per lb.

A frozen joint 4½ lb and under an extra 20 minutes per lb.

A frozen joint over 4½ lb an extra 30 minutes per lb.

The oven temperature is usually maintained from below, so place the cooking pan as near the centre as possible.

how to carve

HOW TO CARVE BEST END NECK OR LOIN

Place rack with the fat side toward the carver. Put fork firmly into meaty section. Cut down between ribs. Lift slices on knife blade, using fork to steady it. Serve each person two rib slices.

HOW TO CARVE BONE-IN SHOULDER

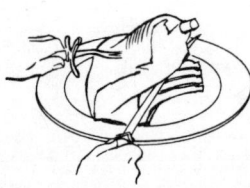

(Unless you are adept at carving, better try this in the kitchen.) Place roast with round bone at carver's right and blade bone towards carver. Cut along ribs and back bone separating meat from bones Remove bones to separate platter.

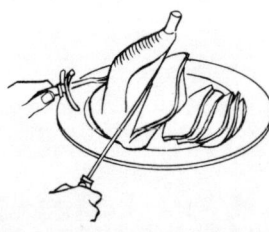

Cut slices from round bone end until blade bone is reached. Remove blade and round bones together by cutting around bones with knife. Remove bones to separate platter. Slice remaining boneless meat.

HOW TO CARVE A LEG

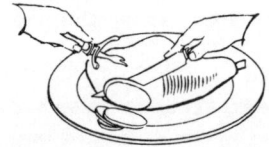

Place leg of lamb with small bone at carver's right and thick meaty portion on far side. Slice off two or three thin, lengthwise slices.

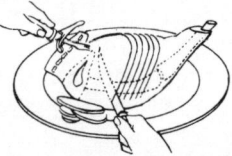

Turn leg to rest on cut surface. Beginning at the base of the bulge, cut down to the bone. Continue cutting thin slices (from right to left).

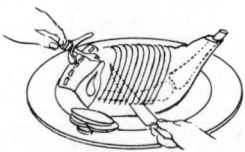

Release slices by cutting underneath along leg bone. Second helpings may be carved from the meat remaining on the leg bone.

Chapter 2

ROASTS, POT ROASTS AND BRAISES

1 THE SOUTH PACIFIC ROAST

A Delicious Family Meal

1 leg lamb, hogget or mutton
salt
pepper

2 tablespoons flour
3 tablespoons fat

Season joint and prepare roasting pan. Pre-heat oven to 350°F, Regulo 4. Place meat in the pan in the centre of the oven and follow timetable on page 17.

When cooked, remove and dish meat. Make the gravy (recipe 170) and serve immediately with mint sauce (recipe 181) or mint jelly (recipe 187), and a choice of vegetables. Roast some of these around the meat : medium-sized onions, portions of potato, pumpkin, parsnip, kumara (sweet potato) or whole and halved tomatoes. Also serve a green vegetable—peas, beans, silver beet or cabbage.
Serves 3 portions per lb.

2 CRUSTY JOINT

1 leg lamb, hogget or mutton
salt
pepper
2 tablespoons flour

3 tablespoons fat
2 tablespoons full cream milk powder
1 tablespoon onion soup powder
2 level tablespoons brown sugar

Season meat and place in the roasting pan. Mix milk and onion soup powders and pat on to the upper surface as topping. Before placing joint in pre-heated oven (350° : Regulo 4) let 2 or 3 minutes lapse to reduce the top heat. About half an hour before the joint is cooked sprinkle topping with brown sugar. Dish joint and prepare gravy (recipe 170). Choose accompanying vegetables from Chapter 19.
Serves 3 portions per lb.

3 MELLOW ROAST

Suitable for any portion of the carcase

5 lb leg or square shoulder of hogget
  or lamb
1 tablespoon flour
onion soup powder (optional)
Seasoned honey: mix the following
3 teaspoons salt
$\frac{1}{4}$ teaspoon pepper
1 clove garlic crushed with salt
$\frac{1}{2}$ teaspoon grated horse-radish or
1 teaspoon horse-radish cream

1 tablespoon peanut oil
4 tablespoons red or white wine
4 tablespoons cream or top milk

2 teaspoons honey
2 teaspoons peanut oil
2 teaspoons lemon juice (lamb) or
cider vinegar (mutton and hogget)

Thoroughly rub joint with seasoned honey mixture and let it stand ½ to 1 hour. Sprinkle the flour (or use half flour and half onion soup powder) in roasting dish and add oil. Put in the joint and cover with firm lid. Pre-heat oven to 400° : Regulo 6.

Hogget : bake ¾ hour : reduce heat to 300° : Regulo 2 and bake another 1¾ hours. MT 182°.

Lamb : bake ¾ hour : reduce heat to 300° : Regulo 2 and bake another 1¼ hours. MT 180°.

When cooked, dish joint and keep warm.

Choose accompanying vegetables from Chapter 19.

Gravy: pour off fat, add red wine (white wine for lamb) to the pan browning, and stir until it boils. Reduce heat and add cream or top milk. Continue stirring until gravy reboils. Check seasoning before serving.

Note: mustard powder may be substituted for horse-radish, in which case, crush the garlic with celery salt.

4 MEADOW SWEET JOINT

Suitable for any lamb, hogget or mutton joint

4 lb shoulder hogget	2 bay leaves
2½ teaspoon salt	1-2 cups milk
good shake pepper	1 large onion
1 clove garlic crushed with salt	
Gravy :	
2 cups stock or water	1 teaspoon salt
1 tablespoon soya sauce	pepper—a generous shake
pinch of sugar	1 tablespoon flour

Season joint. Put bay leaves in a roasting dish, add the joint and pour sufficient milk over it to cover the pan to a depth of about ⅛ inch. Cover the joint with lightly seasoned onion slices and put firm lid on pan. Pre-heat oven to 350° : Regulo 4.

Bake joint about the centre of the oven for approximately 2¼ hours—MT 182° or until it is well cooked. To roast lamb or mutton joints see page 15.

To prepare gravy, remove fat and bay leaves from the liquor. Stir in stock or water, soya sauce, sugar, salt and pepper—boil and blend thickening (the flour mixed with a little cold water until smooth) until the gravy reboils. Reduce heat and simmer ten minutes or longer. Serve in separate dish.

Accompanying vegetables : steamed potatoes in serving-size pieces, purée of steamed carrot and parsnip, and brussels sprouts or buttered cabbage. (Chapter 19).

Serves 7-8.

5 LAMB IN A BLANKET

4 lb shank end leg of lamb boned	1 large egg
2½ teaspoons salt	1¼ lb rough puff pastry (recipe 223) or
¼ teaspoon pepper	1½ lb short pastry (recipe 224)
Savoury breadcrumbs (recipe 197)	White wine sauce (recipe 177)

Prepare 2 cups savoury breadcrumbs, and combine with 2 tablespoons beaten egg. Trim fat from joint and rub inside and out with seasoning. Shape neatly.

Roll pastry about ⅛ inch thick and roll it on to lightly floured rolling pin. Unroll on to a shallow roasting pan. Handle gently and put on a layer of crumb coating, size of joint. Place meat on this, paint with beaten egg and pat remaining coating over it. Carefully lift pastry over joint, trim edges and moisten. Fold one edge over the other and seal neatly, forming a seam. Flute and decorate with pastry leaves, moistening backs to seal in place. Prick in several places with a fork. Bake in oven pre-heated to 450° for 15 minutes. Reduce heat to 325° and bake another 2 hours.

Prepare sauce, garnish with chopped mint.

Accompanying vegetables: small new potatoes and buttered green peas.

Serves 12.

6 BRAISED LAMB SHOULDER WITH PEACH TOPPING

Ideal for electric frying pan

$3\frac{1}{2}$ lb lamb shoulder
$2\frac{1}{4}$ teaspoons salt
$\frac{1}{4}$ teaspoon pepper
$\frac{1}{2}$ teaspoon ground ginger or
1 teaspoon green ginger root grated
1 cup peach syrup

$\frac{1}{2}$-1 tablespoon lemon juice
peach slices
1 tablespoon cream
almonds (optional)
gin (optional)

Season joint and place in pan. Mix ginger, peach syrup and lemon juice (1 tablespoon if the syrup is heavy). Pour syrup over meat and cover firmly. Set frying pan or oven at 200° gas oven Regulo $\frac{1}{2}$. Allow 4 to $4\frac{1}{2}$ hours cooking time. Turn meat after 2 hours. Half an hour before the joint is cooked lift it from the pan. Pour fat from pan juices and stir in cream. Return joint and cover it with peach slices. Place lid on pan and when the liquor has heated baste the fruit topping. When joint is well cooked, remove to serving dish and keep warm. Garnish with almonds slivered and lightly roasted (optional).

To thicken gravy reduce it by rapid boiling and check seasoning.

Serve with purée of potatoes, steamed pumpkin slices or potatoes baked in their jackets, steamed celery with parsley sauce supreme (recipe 179) and buttered green peas.

Note: Canned pears, apricots or pineapple may replace peaches and syrup. Gin to taste may be added to the fruit syrup.

Serves 5.

7 LEMON HONEY SPRING LAMB BRAISE

4 lb leg spring lamb
1 tablespoon flour
1 tablespoon fat
1 clove garlic

$2\frac{1}{2}$ teaspoons salt
$\frac{1}{4}$ teaspoon pepper
2 tablespoons lemon juice
1 tablespoon honey or apricot jam

Put flour and fat in the roasting pan. Crush garlic with salt, add pepper, and lemon juice. Rub into joint and place in pan. Spread the honey or jam on its upper surface. Cover with firm lid. Pre-heat oven to 350°: Regulo 4.

Bake for $1\frac{1}{2}$ hours. Meat thermometer 180°. Joint should be well cooked but be careful not to overcook. Dish and prepare gravy (recipe 170).

Choose vegetables to accompany (Chapter 19).

Note: If hogget or mutton joints are cooked in this way, use 3 tablespoons of cider or wine vinegar instead of the lemon juice; and mint jelly (recipe 187) may replace the honey or apricot jam.

Allow 4 lb hogget joint 2 to $2\frac{1}{4}$ hours. Mutton $2\frac{3}{4}$ to 3 hours.

Serves 6-7.

8 SPRING LAMB WITH WHITE WINE

4 lb spring lamb jointed
2 cloves garlic
6 rosemary leaves
1½ cups medium-dry white wine
Glaze—see Glossary:
2 tablespoons white wine
1 tablespoon honey

2½ teaspoons salt
pepper—freshly ground
soured cream

2 teaspoons lemon juice
1 oz mild cheese

With a sharp pointed knife make six tracks along the bone and insert a sliver of garlic and a bruised leaf of rosemary in each. Put meat in small roasting pan and pour over it 1 cup of wine. Cover and leave to stand about 2 hours—turn and baste frequently. Remove joint and season with salt and a generous shake of pepper. Return to the dish and cover firmly. Pre-heat oven to 350° : Regulo 4. Bake about 1½ hours. Meat thermometer 180°.

Glaze: *As soon as the joint is cooked, place it in a fireproof pan and return to the oven. In a small saucepan put white wine, honey, and lemon juice. As soon as it boils remove from heat. With a sharp knife cut a criss-cross diamond pattern on the upper surface of the joint. Generously apply the hot glaze with a brush or spoon and grate a little mild cheese over it. Place under pre-heated grill (not too close to heat) for a few minutes until the cheese melts and changes colour. Watch carefully while preparing gravy.*

Gravy: *Pour off fat, add ½ cup of wine, stir and let it boil a few seconds. Add a little soured cream (page 135). Reheat and serve.*

or

Make gravy (recipe 170). When it boils add 3 tablespoons of wine and a dash of soured cream a minute or so before serving.

Garnish joint with lemon wedges and chopped parsley or sprigs of water cress. Include creamed sweet corn (canned) as an accompanying vegetable with small new potatoes coated with parsley butter (recipe 192) and green beans. (Chapter 19).
Serves 10-12.

9 HEAVENLY JOINT

Forequarter or Square Shoulder Lamb or Hogget with Mint Dressing
Delicious hot or cold

6 lb forequarter hogget jointed
3½ teaspoons salt
Dressing:
1 egg yolk
2 level teaspoons mustard powder
2 tablespoons vinegar

½ teaspoon pepper
1 or 2 tablespoons flour

2 tablespoons mint jelly or
2 tablespoons sugar
1 rounded teaspoon butter

Beat egg yolk with mustard, and mint jelly or sugar. Stir in vinegar. Add butter and cook in a double boiler until it thickens, stirring at intervals. If the water is boiling rapidly the dressing will thicken in a few minutes. Cool slightly.

Season joint. Sprinkle flour in a baking dish which has a firm lid. With a brush paint a light coating of dressing on the meaty side of joint and place this side down in pan. Apply a generous amount between the jointed chops and riblets and paint the remainder over the rib surface. Cover the dish.

Pre-heat oven to 350° : Regulo 4. Bake lamb joint 2¼ hours ; hogget, 3 hours.

When making the gravy (recipe 170) omit sugar from the seasoning and instead add a dash of cider vinegar and mint jelly to taste.

Vegetables: Potatoes in serving-size pieces or purée, steamed portions of parsnip coated with parsley butter, and brussels sprouts or buttered cabbage. (Chapter 19).

Serves 3 portions per lb.

10 LEG OF MUTTON BRAISED WITH BEER

6 lb leg of mutton
3¼ teaspoons salt
1 teaspoon pepper
1 tablespoon vinegar
1¼ tablespoons brown sugar

2½ teaspoons mustard
2 cloves garlic crushed with salt
½ teaspoon dried rosemary
1 pint light beer or cider
½ cup of soured cream

Thoroughly rub the mutton with the mixture of salt, garlic, pepper, brown sugar, mustard, rosemary, and vinegar. Leave it on a large plate at least 3 hours, or preferably in the refrigerator overnight.

Pre-heat oven to 425°: Regulo 7. Roast uncovered until the meat is lightly browned (about 45 minutes if straight from the refrigerator). Pour over the warmed beer, firmly cover the dish and reduce heat to 250°: Regulo 1. Bake another 3½ to 4 hours, until tender. Keep joint hot on serving dish.

Pour fat from gravy and stir in soured cream (page 135). Heat thoroughly and check seasoning before serving.

Serve with steamed potatoes, carrots and buttered spinach. (Chapter 19). Serves 12.

11 CARAMELISED LEG OR SHOULDER MUTTON OR HOGGET BRAISE

5 lb shank end leg of mutton or
a boned leg
3 teaspoons salt
¼ teaspoon pepper
1 teaspoon curry powder
1 teaspoon mustard
1 tablespoon flour
6 tablespoons honey
3 tablespoons butter
1 onion

¼ lb prunes or dried apricots
1 apple
1 cup beer
1 cup stock
1 teaspoon green ginger root crushed or
1 teaspoon ground ginger
2 tablespoons tomato sauce
1 tablespoon lemon juice
a little lemon rind
½ cup soured cream

Season joint with mixture of salt, pepper, curry powder, mustard, and flour. In a large heavy-based saucepan melt the honey and butter, stirring until it changes colour (be careful not to burn). Add sliced onion and brown lightly. Then add chopped fruit. Lift out onion and fruit with a slotted spoon and brown the meat, then remove it while you stir in beer, stock, ginger, tomato sauce, lemon juice and rind. Reduce heat, return meat, spread fruit and onion mix on top. If necessary use brown paper to jam the lid firmly on saucepan and simmer slowly on top of stove until tender. Allow hogget 35 to 40 minutes per lb and mutton 45 to 50 minutes per lb.

Remove meat to serving dish, pour off the fat (soak up the remainder with paper tablenapkin). Add soured cream (glossary), check seasoning and let gravy reboil before serving in separate dish.

Vegetables to accompany: purée of potatoes, potatoes baked in their jackets, steamed sliced carrot and buttered green peas. Serves 3 portions per lb.

12 CHRISTMAS ROAST WITH RED WINE STUFFING

5 lb leg hogget boned
3 teaspoons salt
¼ teaspoon pepper
1 clove garlic crushed with salt
2 teaspoons honey

2 teaspoons lemon juice
2 tablespoons flour
3 tablespoons bacon fat
bacon rashers
2 tablespoons red wine
stuffing *

Remove excess fat from cavity. Mix salt, pepper, garlic, honey and lemon juice and well season joint including the cavity (sparingly). Let it stand while preparing stuffing (recipe 198). Fill meat cavity fairly loosely and with a large needle and thread (raffia is suitable) sew up openings using a lacing pattern. Weigh stuffed joint.

Pre-heat oven to 350°: Regulo 4. Put flour and fat in baking dish and heat in oven until sizzling hot. Add joint, baste well wth hot fat and roast approximately 35 minutes per lb. Meat thermometer 182°. Fifteen to twenty minutes before the joint is cooked, top with bacon rashers (rinds removed) and bake (uncovered) until crisp. Place joint on serving dish, remove thread and keep hot.

Make gravy (recipe 170). When it is boiling hard, add red wine. Reduce heat and allow to simmer slowly for at least 10 minutes. Serve separately. Mint or red currant jelly should also accompany this dish. Choose breadsauce (recipe 180) for special occasion.

Roast in serving sizes: onions, pumpkin slices and tomato halves, all seasoned. Steam potatoes to puree or small whole new ones and coat with parsley butter (recipe 192). Also include buttered green peas or green beans. (Chapter 19).

Serves 4 portions per lb.

Note: The red wine in the gravy may be replaced by 1 tablespoon of cider or wine vinegar. A little cream may be added a minute or so before serving.

13 CANTONESE ROAST

5 lb leg hogget
2 teaspoons salt

¼ teaspoon pepper—freshly ground

Mixture for slits:
1 clove garlic crushed
1 tablespoon soya sauce

2 teaspoons honey or brown sugar
2 teaspoons gin or rice wine

Baste:
1 teaspoon salt
1 tablespoon honey

2 tablespoons cider vinegar
2 tablespoons soya sauce

Rub meat with seasoning.

Using a sharp-pointed knife make 6 slits from the under-surface of the leg almost to the upper skin, which must not be pierced. Open each slit with knife, and spoon in mixture. Plug with tinfoil.

Pre-heat oven to 400°. Put joint in the baking pan, slit side up. Paint with baste and roast ½ hour. Baste again and reduce heat to 300°. Allow 35 minutes per pound.

Turn meat half an hour before it is cooked. Paint well with baste and repeat after 10 minutes. Meat thermometer should read 182°-185°, when the joint will be cooked to perfection.

Remove plugs and place on serving dish. Make gravy (recipe 170). Check seasoning.

Vegetable accompaniments: steamed potatoes in serving-size portions, sliced carrots, leeks topped with foundation sauce (recipe 171), grilled tomatoes or puree.(Chapter 19).Garnish with chopped parsley.
Serves 3 portions per lb.
Note: *Brandy may replace gin.*

14 SEARED ROAST OF SPRING LAMB

4 lb leg of lamb	$\frac{1}{4}$ teaspoon pepper
2$\frac{1}{2}$ teaspoons salt	1 cup stock or water
1 clove garlic	a little cream

Chop and mash garlic with salt and pepper and season joint.
Pre-heat oven to 500°. Place meat in a shallow roasting pan above the centre of the oven for 20 to 25 minutes. Then move pan on to a low rack and cover with a square of tinfoil (do not seal). The edges should be an inch or more above the pan base. Reduce temperature to 325°. Roast for a further 1 hour 40 minutes. Meat thermometer 180°. Lift on to a serving dish and keep warm.
Pour all fat from pan. Add cold stock or water, stir up any brown bits and bring to boil. Simmer 2 or 3 minutes. Season to taste. Stir in cream and reheat before serving in a separate dish.
Lift off tinfoil and serve with mint sauce (recipe 181), new potatoes garnished with chopped olives, sautéed mushrooms, buttered green peas, and grilled tomato halves. (Chapter 19).
Serves 3 portions per lb.

15 ROAST LAMB OR HOGGET WITH FRENCH MUSTARD COATING

6 lb of hogget	$\frac{1}{4}$ teaspoon pepper
4 tablespoons french mustard (recipe 185)	1 clove garlic
1 tablespoon soya sauce	1$\frac{1}{2}$ cups stock or water
1 teaspoon rosemary leaves	$\frac{1}{2}$ teaspoon sugar
or $\frac{1}{2}$ teaspoon ground rosemary or thyme	2 tablespoons cream
$\frac{1}{4}$ teaspoon powdered ginger	2 teaspoons cider vinegar
3 teaspoons salt	

Mix mustard, soya sauce, finely chopped rosemary and ginger. Crush garlic with salt and pepper. About 2 hours before required, season joint and paint with mustard mix.
Pre-heat oven to 250°. Place joint in a shallow pan and roast 4 hours. Or, pre-heat oven to 350°, place joint on a low rack, cover and bake about 3 hours. Meat thermometer 182°.
To prepare gravy: pour all fat from pan. Add 1$\frac{1}{2}$ cups of cold stock or water. Stir well while boiling and simmer at least 2 minutes. Season to taste with salt, pepper and $\frac{1}{2}$ teaspoon sugar. Mix 2 teaspoons cider vinegar, 1 teaspoon soya sauce and 2 tablespoons of cream together. Stir in and reheat before serving.
Accompanying vegetables: steamed potato portions, purée of carrot and parsnip, buttered cabbage. (Chapter 19).
Serves 3 portions per lb.

16 LEG OF MUTTON WITH RED WINE MARINADE

Delicate fare

6 lb leg mutton	3½ teaspoons salt
6 cloves	¼ teaspoon pepper
2 cloves garlic	2 tablespoons flour
1 tablespoon lemon juice	2 tablespoons butter
2 cups red wine	1 tablespoon honey

With sharp-pointed knife make tracks in joint, especially along the bone, and insert 6 garlic slivers. Put joint in dish just large enough to hold it. Pour mixture of cloves, lemon juice and wine over the joint, baste and turn frequently. Marinate 12-24 hours. Keep joint covered in a cool safe or in the refrigerator in warm weather.

Pre-heat oven to 275° : Regulo 1½. Drain joint and sprinkle with salt and pepper. Put flour, butter and honey in a roasting pan and melt in the oven for a minute. Be careful not to burn. Stir in the remaining marinade. If necessary add a little more wine to provide sufficient baste and let it come to the boil.

Place joint in the pan, baste well with the hot wine and cover with a firm lid. Cook as high in the oven as possible. Baste 2 or 3 times. Braise 3¾ hours. Meat thermometer 185°.

Remove fat and cloves before making the gravy (recipe 170). The flavour of the wine liquor is really delicious. Accompanying vegetables: small new potatoes, sautéed mushrooms, tomatoes grilled or puréed, buttered green peas or beans. As a garnish use finely shredded raw green peppers.

If possible serve the same red wine at room temperature with this meal.

Serves 3 portions per lb.

To braise a smaller joint see timetable (Chapter 1).

17 MUTTON, HOGGET OR LAMB WITH APRICOT BUTTER

(All measures should be level, and meat must be at room temperature.)

4 lb leg or shoulder lamb	3 tablespoons butter
2½ teaspoons salt	1 tablespoon lemon juice
pepper—a generous shake	1½ teaspoons flour
2 teaspoons monosodium glutamate	1 clove garlic
1½ teaspoons mustard powder	4 tablespoons apricot or peach jam
Sauce :	
1½ tablespoons flour	2 teaspoons apricot or peach jam
1 teaspoon salt	lemon juice or cider vinegar
pepper—a generous shake	

Put salt, pepper, monosodium glutinate, mustard, butter, lemon juice, and flour in a bowl and beat until creamy. Use a fork to beat in the crushed garlic and jam. Coat the under surface of the lamb with half the mixture and place joint this side up in the baking dish. Cover firmly.

Pre-heat oven to 300° : Regulo 2. Bake about the centre of the oven. Allow a lamb joint approximately 1¾ hours, hogget 2¼-2½ hours, and mutton 3¼-3½ hours. At half time insert meat thermometer, turn the joint, and spread with the remaining mustard mixture. Replace cover and continue roasting until tender. MT 180°. Keep warm on serving dish.

Sauce: Put 1½ tablespoons of fat from the pan in a small saucepan over low heat. Pour off all the remaining fat and add about 2 cups of water to the roasting pan, stir well, and scrape up the pan browning. Boil a few minutes, then leave to cool slightly.

Into the sizzling fat in saucepan blend flour until no lumps remain. *Add salt, pepper and jam.* Stir in stock from roasting dish, a little at a time, and continue stirring until sauce boils—reduce heat and simmer at least 10 minutes. Add a squeeze of lemon juice or dash of cider vinegar to taste.

Alternative: *Make gravy (recipe 170).* Add a tablespoon of jam and a squeeze of lemon juice or cider vinegar to taste.

Accompanying vegetables : potato portions, parsnip purée, sliced carrots (top these with a little parsley butter), and buttered broad beans.

Serves 3 portions per lb.

18 SHANK END LEG OF MUTTON WITH LAGER SAUCE

Suitable for fresh or salt mutton

A deep wide bowl without a lid and a larger saucepan with a firm lid are essential. A boned and rolled joint will fit a smaller bowl.

4 lb shank end of mutton	pinch of sugar
2½ teaspoons salt (for fresh mutton only)	2 medium-sized onions
2 cloves garlic	1 rib celery with some greentop
pepper—a generous shake	1 large carrot
1½ tablespoons flour	2 large tomatoes or ½ cup of puree
2 teaspoons golden syrup	lager sauce (recipe 176)

Have joint boned and remove excess fat from cavity before rolling. Chop and mash garlic with salt, add pepper and flour and season joint. Paint one side with golden syrup (heat a little in cold weather). Slice one onion into the bottom of the bowl, and place joint, painted surface down, on this. Apply remaining syrup.

Sit the uncovered bowl in a saucepan containing sufficient boiling water to reach half-way up the bowl. Put firm lid on the saucepan. Keep water boiling steadily and replenish when necessary. Do not put any water in the bowl.

Steam mutton approximately 3 hours, hogget 2½ to 2¾ hours, and lamb about 2 hours. Meat must be tender but avoid overcooking.

Half an hour before joint is cooked remove saucepan from heat for a minute, and carefully lift out bowl. Pour fat (reserve 3 tablespoons) from liquor, and soak up residue with paper table napkin. Slice onion, celery, carrot and tomatoes. Season with ½ teaspoon salt, a pinch of sugar and a generous shake of pepper and arrange them round the meat. Return bowl to the boiling water and re-cover saucepan. When cooked put joint on a plate and keep it warm. Strain vegetables and retain liquor.

Prepare lager sauce.

Joint may be carved at table and sauce served in separate dish. Alternatively carve meat and arrange slices on a serving dish. Cover with sauce and garnish with chopped parsley and lemon slices.

Serve with potato purée, and buttered cabbage.

Serves 3 servings per lb.

Note: To re-serve, heat remaining meat slices very slowly in the left-over sauce.

19 HOGGET FLAP, STUFFED AND BRAISED

1 flap boned
1½ teaspoons salt
pepper

stuffing (recipe 197)
1 teaspoon honey
1 cup milk

Trim excess fat and any rough edges from meat. Season inner surface lightly with salt and pepper. Prepare savoury breadcrumb stuffing, using only 1 cup of breadcrumbs and 1 teaspoon of celery salt. Spread over seasoned meat surface, roll and secure (glossary). Weigh joint. Rub with remaining salt and spread with honey. Place in casserole. Pour over the milk and sprinkle with pepper. Put on firm lid and bake about 1½ hours in oven pre-heated to 350° : Regulo 4. Joint should be well cooked. Dish joint and prepare gravy (recipe 170). Vegetables as accompaniment : steamed potatoes in serving-size pieces or small new ones, purée of carrot and parsnip, buttered silver beet or spinach. (Chapter 19). Garnish with chopped parsley.
Serves 4 servings per lb.

20 CROWN ROAST OF LAMB OR HOGGET
(See definition, Chapter 1.)

Description—page *14.*

Order joint in advance.
1 crown roast
2 teaspoons salt
1 clove garlic

pepper—freshly ground
1 tablespoon flour
tinfoil

Chop garlic and mash with salt. Add pepper and flour and season the inside of crown and between joints. To avoid charring the sawn rib ends (top of joint) protect with tinfoil or paste balls.
Pre-heat oven to 350° : Regulo 4. Place a trivet or a low wire rack in a shallow pan about the centre of oven. Stand roast, protected rib ends down, on this. Allow lamb approximately 1½ hours, hogget 2 hours.
Place on serving dish with cutlets at base and keep warm. Make gravy (recipe 170). Remove the centre string encircling the joint, also tinfoil or paste balls. Decorate rib ends with slices of stuffed olives, wedges of vegetables or paper frills.
Joint may be served as is, and with mint sauce. The cavity may be filled with steamed cauliflower (Chapter 19) topped with white foundation sauce (recipe 171) and sprinkled with either buttered breadcrumbs, grated cheese, or grated boiled egg and chopped parsley.
Accompanying vegetables : purée of potatoes, grilled tomatoes, buttered cabbage or green peas. (Chapter 19).
If joint is served cold, fill cavity with attractive green salad and camouflage rib ends with wedges of firm fruit or vegetables used in the salad. Serve mayonnaise or french dressing separately.
Serves 6 to 7.

21 CROWN ROAST WITH SAVOURY STUFFING

Delicious either hot or cold

1 crown roast lamb or hogget
2½ teaspoons salt
1 clove garlic
pepper—freshly ground

1 tablespoon flour
tinfoil
stuffing (recipe 198)
1 egg

Season and prepare joint for roasting as in recipe 20.

Prepare stuffing using a beaten egg to mix instead of the wine. Put a round of tinfoil on trivet or wire rack and place in roasting pan. On this place joint with the cutlets or riblets at the base. Loosely fill cavity with stuffing, and cover with more tinfoil. Pre-heat oven to 350° : Regulo 4. Allow lamb 2 hours and hogget 2½ hours.

To lift joint on to serving dish, tip slightly, put fish slice in position and give support from a protected hand. Keep joint warm and prepare gravy (recipe 170).

Suggested garnishes for stuffing are : bacon rashers grilled until crisp and then crumbled, or sliced or grated hard boiled egg, or grated cheese and a sprinkling of chopped parsley. Decorate rib ends (recipe 20).

Accompanying vegetables: small new potatoes, baby carrots, both coated with parsley butter, celery or marrow topped with foundation sauce, buttered green peas or green beans (Chapter 19).

Serve cold joint surrounded with salad greens with mayonnaise or french dressing as accompaniment.

Include either mint sauce (recipe 181), mint jelly (recipe 187) or red currant jelly (recipe 186) as a side-dish.

Serves 8.

Chapter 3

POACHED OR BOILED HOGGET OR MUTTON JOINTS

This process merits wider recognition and is suitable for a leg, shoulder or square shoulder, rolled loin or flap, shank or Spanish neck. Totally immerse meat in cold seasoned liquor, bring it to boiling point, but not to a full boil. Reduce heat and slowly simmer. Cover saucepan firmly. If necessary jam the lid on with brown paper.

When adding wine, beer, or cider to the poaching liquor, for economical reasons choose a receptacle just large enough to hold the joint. If joint is boned and firmly rolled, choose a larger vessel and add bones to stock. Allow 40-45 minutes per lb total cooking time. Allow these joints to cool up to 12 hours in the liquor. This improves the flavour of cold meat but it is important to observe this time-limit.

When cold the fat can be easily removed. Use the strained liquor as a stock or soup base. Store in refrigerator.

22 MUTTON JOINT POACHED WITH VINEGAR

To each quart of water add:

1 large onion	4 branches parsley
1 carrot	1 sprig rosemary
2 ribs celery	2 bayleaves
4 cloves garlic	2 teaspoons honey or brown sugar
6 or 8 bacon rinds	2 tablespoons vinegar
2½ teaspoons salt	12 peppercorns

Chop onion, carrot and celery. Chop and crush garlic with salt. Knot bacon rinds. Bruise herbs and tie with cotton into bouquet garni. If unavailable use 1 teaspoon mixed herbs.
Put mutton joint with all ingredients in a heavy-based saucepan. The cold liquor should just cover the meat. Bring to boiling point. Cover and reduce heat to a low simmer. Cook 40-45 minutes per lb or until tender. Serve with caper sauce (recipe 172) or prepare parsley sauce supreme (recipe 179), omitting the salt and using the fat-free cooking liquor (strained) instead of the milk. Add a little cream before serving.
Note: *This recipe, with salt omitted, is also suitable for salt or pickled joints*

23 MUTTON JOINT POACHED WITH MILK

To 1 pint of water and 1 pint of milk add:

1 large onion	a good pinch mace
8 cloves	2 tablespoons soya sauce
2-3 bay leaves	8 peppercorns
1 rib of celery	2 teaspoons salt
3 branches of parsley	parsley sauce supreme (recipe 178)
1 teaspoon nutmeg	cream

Halve onion and stud with cloves. Tie bay leaves, celery and parsley into bouquet garni. Put meat and all ingredients except parsley sauce and cream into a heavy-based saucepan. Follow the method in recipe 22. Prepare sauce using all or part of strained cooking liquor as stock instead of milk (omit salt). Add a little cream and check seasoning. Serve joint topped with sauce or first carve it and arrange slices on a serving dish. To re-serve, very slowly reheat sliced mutton in parsley sauce.

24 MUTTON JOINT POACHED IN BEER OR CIDER

1 pint light beer or cider and 1 pint stock or water:

2 tablespoons lemon juice	1 tablespoon honey
2 teaspoons mustard powder	12 peppercorns
3 cloves garlic	3 bay leaves
2 teaspoons salt	parsley branches
1 onion	1 sprig rosemary
6 bacon rinds	1 sprig thyme or 1 teaspoon dried mixed herbs

Mix lemon juice and mustard. Chop and crush garlic with salt. Slice onion. Knot bacon rinds together. Tie bay leaves, rosemary, thyme and parsley into bouquet garni. Put joint and all ingredients in a heavy-based saucepan and follow the method in recipe 22. Serve with mustard sauce (recipe 175) or follow recipe 171 for white foundation sauce, using strained liquor to replace milk and a little soured cream before serving.

25 HOGGET OR MUTTON POACHED IN DRY RED WINE

Delicious served cold with salad

To one pint water and one pint wine add:

large onion	juice and grated rind of lemon
2 ribs celery	a little bruised green ginger root
2 cloves garlic	1 bay leaf
2 teaspoons salt	$\frac{1}{2}$ teaspoon coriander—or mixed herbs
$\frac{1}{4}$ cup mint or red currant jelly	8 peppercorns
	red wine sauce (recipe 177)

Chop onion and celery. Crush garlic with salt. Put all ingredients except sauce in heavy-based saucepan.

Follow method in recipe 22 for a hot joint. Prepare sauce (recipe 177), replacing soup powder stock and $\frac{1}{2}$ the wine with $1\frac{1}{4}$ cups strained fat-free stock and $\frac{1}{4}$ cup red wine, omit salt. Serve separately, or slice meat and arrange on a serving dish, top with sauce and sprinkle with chopped parsley.

26 POACHED, SALT OR PICKLED MUTTON OR MUTTON HAM

Joint, salt or pickled	1 carrot
beer and water in equal parts or	1 small turnip
water plus 2 tablespoons vinegar	12 peppercorns
2 large onions	3 bay leaves
8 cloves	1 tablespoon golden syrup

Soak joint in cold water for about 2 hours.

Halve onions and stud with cloves. Slice carrot and dice turnip. Put joint with all ingredients in a heavy-based saucepan. Just cover with liquid. Bring to boil. Reduce heat. Cover and simmer until the meat is tender. Serve hot with either mustard sauce (recipe 175) or parsley sauce supreme (recipe 179).

Return remainder of joint to liquor up to 12 hours. Remove fat, drain and serve cold with salads.

Chapter 4

TO GRILL, SAUTE, AND BAKE LAMB, HOGGET AND MUTTON

To Grill: To cook quickly fairly close to direct heat from above or below the meat. Hot coals should be at required temperature. (See Chapter 5, Barbecues).

To Broil: To cook meat in the oven on a mesh frame using dry heat. The hot air then surrounds the meat. In America "broil" is equivalent to our "grill".

To Sauté: To fry in a small quantity of hot butter, cooking oil or fat.

To Deep fry: To cook in deep fat pre – heated to a high temperature (glossary).

Unless stated otherwise, cuts for all purposes should be at room temperature. Lamb, hogget or mutton steaks are cut about $\frac{3}{4}$ inch thick from the fillet or butt end of leg, preferably boned. Use a sharp knife to slice steaks across the grain. Trim off any rough bits and excess fat. Nick steaks in several places round edges to prevent curling.

Lamb and hogget cutlets (page 130) for grilling are sectioned from best end neck. Chops are usually from the loin. Grill or sauté lamb or hogget as cutlets.

Mutton cutlets, chops and steaks: pound with a meat mallet or rolling pin to break down the meat fibres and reduce thickness before tenderising in a marinade (Chapter 18).
Grilling method: Pre-heat grill 4-5 minutes.
Allow: 1 teaspoon salt per lb of meat.
      1 teaspoon honey per lb of meat.
      pepper—freshly ground.

Variations: One or more of the following may be added to the honey: a drop or two of garlic juice or substitute, $\frac{1}{2}$ to 1 teaspoon mustard powder, 1 teaspoon butter, a small pinch of dried marjoram or rosemary.

Arrange cutlets, chops or steaks on grilling rack in a shallow drip pan. Sprinkle surface with half the salt and lightly smear with half the honey, especially the fatty areas. Place 2 to 5 inches from maximum heat. For mutton grills, if the space is available, allow 6 inches.

Timing depends largely upon the distance from heat, which in turn depends upon the thickness and age of the meat.

When the fatty tissue is brown and just crisp, turn, season and grill as before. Sprinkle generously with pepper. If served immediately the meats will be moist and cooked to perfection. The fat will be in the drip pan and the fatty tissue remaining will be crisp and palatable.

27 PAT'S DEVIL GRILL

6 hogget loin chops or 2 lb steaks   pepper—a good shake
2 teaspoons salt   Pat's Devil topping (recipe 183)

Pre-heat grill.
Arrange chops on grilling rack. Sprinkle with half the salt and pepper. Put rack in drip pan and place meat under grill, if possible 4 inches from heat. Turn when fatty tissue is nicely brown and crisp.
Sprinkle with remaining seasoning and return to grill. When brown, spread with Pat's Devil topping. Return to grill for a minute or so until the topping is sizzling. Garnish with parsley or watercress sprigs. Serves 6.

28 PAT'S GRILLED CHOPS WITH OYSTERS

6 lamb or hogget chops
salt
pepper
1 dozen fresh oysters and liquor

freshly ground pepper
1 teaspoon lemon juice
1 teaspoon sherry

Follow recipe 27 to season and grill chops.
Put oysters, pepper, lemon juice and sherry in pan. Simmer over very low heat until the
oysters plump. Remove immediately. Pour over chops and serve garnished with lemon
slices and parsley sprigs.
Serves 6.

29 GRILLED NOISETTES WITH PINEAPPLE

6 lamb or hogget loin chops boned
1 teaspoon honey
1 teaspoon mustard powder
1 teaspoon butter
1 clove garlic
2 teaspoons salt
generous pinch freshly ground pepper

2 teaspoons lemon juice
$\frac{1}{2}$ cup pineapple juice
2 tablespoons butter
1 can pineapple rings
1 tablespoon chopped mint
6 maraschino cherries (optional)
toothpicks

To form noisettes remove excess fat from chops. Roll each end round eye of meat and secure
firmly with toothpick.
Mix honey, mustard, butter, garlic, crushed with salt, pepper, lemon juice and 2 teaspoons
pineapple juice. Spread chops evenly with the mixed seasoning and let them stand 10 to
20 minutes. In a small pan put remaining pineapple juice and the butter. Stir and boil rapidly
until reduced to almost half quantity. Watch carefully or the juice will evaporate. Remove
from heat, add mint and keep warm.
Pre-heat grill. Place noisettes on rack in drip pan and grill each side about 10 to 15 minutes
or until the fatty tissue is crisp and brown. Paint with pineapple baste, sprinkle with pepper
and place a drained ring of pineapple on each noisette. Baste and grill until sizzling. Turn
pineapple, baste generously and grill another minute or so. Serve with a maraschino cherry
in each pineapple ring.
Canned peach halves and juice may substitute for pineapple.
Serves 6.

30 SAVOURY GRILL

Hogget or lamb cutlets, loin chops or steak

Allow per lb:
1 teaspoon mustard
1 teaspoon honey
pinch marjoram
1 tablespoon tomato sauce

1 teaspoon cooking oil
1 teaspoon garlic salt
pepper

Mix all ingredients except pepper. Rub into each side of chops or steak and stand 10 to 20
minutes in a pile.
Pre-heat grill. Place meat on rack in drip pan and grill until the fatty tissue is brown and
crisp. Serve sprinkled with freshly ground pepper.

31 SPRING LAMB CUTLETS OR STEAK WITH ROSEMARY

Allow per lb:
1 clove garlic
¼ teaspoon rosemary leaves or
   pinch of the dried herb

1 teaspoon honey
1 teaspoon salt
pepper

Chop and crush garlic and rosemary with salt, and rub into cutlets. Smear with honey and grill each side (4 to 5 minutes) until fatty tissue is brown and just crisp. Apply a generous grinding of black pepper, and serve with parsley butter balls (recipe 192).

32 DEVILLED LEG MUTTON CHOPS OR STEAK

4 leg chops about ¾ inch thick
½ cup cider vinegar
1 teaspoon mustard powder
cayenne pepper
2 tablespoons butter
1½ teaspoons salt

freshly ground pepper
chilli powder (or cayenne)
1 teaspoon mustard
2 tablespoons soya sauce
1 tablespoon peach, mango or apple
   chutney

Marinate chops in mixture of cider vinegar, mustard and a pinch of cayenne pepper for 6 to 8 hours. Turn several times. Mix softened (not melted) butter with the remaining ingredients. Chilli powder to taste.
Drain and dry chops. Thinly spread one side of each chop with a little of the mixture. Place on rack, treated side up, 4 to 5 inches from pre-heated grill. When nicely browned, turn, and with a very sharp knife score surface to about half its depth. Evenly spread the remaining butter mixture and grill until the fatty tissue is brown and just crisp. Chops must not be dry or overcooked.
Serve with red pepper sauce, or your favourite barbecue sauce.
Serves 4.

33 SAUTEED LAMB CUTLETS

Suitable for steak, cutlets or chops

1-2 cutlets or equivalent steak per serving
1 teaspoon salt
1 clove garlic
1 teaspoon honey
butter or peanut oil

flour
pepper—freshly ground
2 tablespoons lemon juice or medium-dry
   white wine
chives or parsley (garnish) 1 teaspoon

Chop and crush garlic with salt and mix with honey (sufficient to season 1 lb of meat).
Heat a little butter in frying pan until it starts to brown. Pound cutlets or steaks. Remove excess fat. Spread seasoning evenly over meat and sprinkle with flour. Sauté 3 minutes each side, less if preferred underdone. Place on serving dish, sprinkle generously with pepper and keep warm. Pour fat from pan. Melt 1 tablespoon of butter and add lemon juice or white wine. Scrape up pan browning. Boil a few seconds and spoon over cutlets. Serve garnished with chopped chives or parsley.

34 PAPER THIN STEAK

1 lb hogget steak
1 tablespoon peanut oil
1 tablespoon butter
1 teaspoon salt
1 clove garlic
1 small onion

1 teaspoon monosodium glutamate
  (optional)
pepper—freshly ground
chives
1 lemon (garnish)

Heat oil and butter until very hot. Slice steaks paper-thin. Nick edges and season with garlic crushed with salt and glutamate. Sauté sliced onion and when lightly brown move aside and sauté steaks until the colour changes—barely ½ a minute each side. Serve generously sprinkled with pepper and chopped chives. Garnish with lemon slices.
Serves 4.

35 HOGGET SCHNITZELS (I)

1 lb hogget rump steak
1 teaspoon salt
flour
1 egg
¼ teaspoon pepper

Marinade: mix
½ cup milk
1 clove garlic crushed
1 bay leaf

1 tablespoon peanut or corn oil
breadcrumbs
1 tablespoon butter
1 lemon (garnish)

pinch grated nutmeg
parsley stalks crushed

Slice steaks ¼ inch thick and firmly roll with rolling pin. Remove excess fat. Marinate for 2 hours. Drain, sprinkle with salt and flour. Beat together egg, pepper, 1 teaspoon cooking oil and 1 tablespoon marinade. Dip steaks in mixture, coat with breadcrumbs and let lie a few minutes until firm. Sauté in hot butter and oil until each side is crisp and golden brown. Garnish with lemon slices.
Serves 4.

36 HOGGET SCHNITZELS (II)

1 lb hogget rump steak
2 apples
1 teaspoon salt

pepper
flour
2 tablespoons butter

Slice steaks ¼ inch thick, and firmly roll with rolling pin. Remove excess fat and spread with generous amount of freshly grated apple. Pile one on top of the other in a mason jar lying on its side. Screw on lid and keep in refrigerator 12 to 24 hours.
Sprinkle with salt, pepper and flour. The egg and breadcrumbs coating in Hogget Schnitzel (I) is optional. Sauté in hot butter until each side is crisp and golden brown.
Serves 4.
Note: *For egg – dip, beat 1 egg with 1 tablespoon top milk or cream.*

37 JANET'S LAMB STEAK OR CUTLETS

Tender steak or cutlets
black peppercorns
peanut oil
butter

1 teaspoon salt
cream
parsley (garnish)
lemon (garnish)

Slice steak or cutlets ½ inch thick. Trim excess fat and pound with meat mallet or rolling pin. Thickly cover both sides with freshly ground pepper. Leave for several hours. Smear heavy-based pan with oil. When really hot, add steaks and turn several times—takes about 7 minutes to brown.

Remove to serving dish and keep hot. Pour any fat from pan and add 1½ tablespoons butter per lb of meat. Heat until it changes colour and add 1 teaspoon salt and 1 tablespoon cream. Stir and cook slowly a minute or so. Spread over steaks and serve garnished with lemon slices and parsley or watercress sprigs. Include a green salad with accompaniments.

38 LAMB OR HOGGET CUTLETS OR STEAKS ANGLAISE

6 cutlets
1 clove garlic
1½ teaspoons salt
pepper
1½ tablespoons flour
1 egg

a shake of Worcester sauce
1 or 2 tablespoons milk
breadcrumbs
parsley
lemon

Chop and crush garlic with salt and put in plastic bag with generous pinch of pepper and the flour. Shake to mix.

Remove excess fat from cutlets and beat to flatten a little. Put in the bag one at a time and shake to cover completely with seasoning (use all of it). Dip in mixture of egg beaten with Worcester sauce, milk, and a pinch of pepper and salt. Coat with breadcrumbs. Place a sheet of greaseproof paper in baking dish. Put crumbed cutlets on this. Fold to cover completely but do not seal. Pre-heat oven to 450°. Place in middle of oven and bake about ½ hour, or until crumbs are crisp and golden. Lift from parcel on to grilling rack, stand rack in pan and return to oven for two or three minutes.

Serve garnished with parsley sprigs and lemon slices.

Note: *The cutlets or steaks may be sautéed in equal parts of hot oil and butter for 10 to 12 minutes each side, until golden brown and crisp. If necessary reduce heat a little to make sure they are well cooked.*

Serves 6.

39 SCALLOPED CUTLETS

Suitable for lamb or hogget cutlets, steaks or riblets

6 cutlets
1 clove garlic
1½ teaspoons salt
1½ tablespoons flour
generous shake pepper

coating sauce (recipe 173)
breadcrumbs
butter
peanut oil

Remove excess fat from cutlets. Chop and crush garlic with salt and put in plastic bag with flour and pepper. Shake to mix. Add cutlets one at a time and shake until completely covered with seasoning (use all of it).

Prepare sauce and let it cool a little. Spread on one side of seasoned cutlets and turn on to breadcrumbs. Cover with remaining sauce and coat with crumbs.

Heat 1 tablespoon each of butter and oil in pan until sizzling. Sauté cutlets 10 to 12 minutes each side until well cooked, golden and crisp. Read note, Recipe 38.

Serves 6.

40 PAM'S HOGGET LOIN CHOPS

Hogget loin chops (1 per serving)

Allow per lb:

1 clove garlic	bacon rashers
1 teaspoon salt	chutney
pepper	toothpicks
pinch dried dill (optional)	

Season both sides of chops with mixture of crushed garlic, salt, pepper and dill, spread with strong chutney and wrap each chop in a rasher of bacon. Secure with toothpicks.

Pre-heat oven to 450°. Bake on a grilling rack, approximately 30 to 35 minutes for chops $\frac{3}{4}$ inch thick.

41 FOOD FOR THE GODS

Lamb or hogget middle neck chops or cutlets with red wine stuffing

8 chops	2 cups savoury breadcrumbs (recipe 197)
1 clove garlic	flour
$1\frac{1}{2}$ teaspoons salt	egg
$\frac{1}{4}$ teaspoon pepper	1 tablespoon cream or top milk
$1\frac{1}{2}$ teaspoons honey	bacon rashers
2 tablespoons red wine	

Trim and flatten chops. Rub each side with garlic crushed with salt and pepper. Spread with the honey mixed with 1 tablespoon wine and leave to stand in a pile about $\frac{1}{2}$ hour.

To 1 cup savoury breadcrumbs add 1 tablespoon wine and gently lift to mix. Put chops on floured surface and arrange stuffing on half of them. Sandwich with remaining chops, unfloured surface to stuffing—press gently and tie each pair in two places. If necessary sprinkle with more flour, dip in beaten egg and cream mixture and coat all over with savoury breadcrumbs. Place greaseproof paper in baking pan, put chops on this and form a parcel. Do not seal completely.

Pre-heat oven to 425°. Place in the middle of oven if heat is from below. Allow middle neck chops about $1\frac{1}{2}$ hours. Lamb cutlets (best end neck) 40 to 45 minutes. Hogget cutlets 1 hour. If necessary to crisp before serving, place on a rack under grill—not too close to heat—for a minute or two. Remove the threads. Serve each pair of chops topped with a bacon rasher grilled until crisp.

Note: For loin chops, make a pocket in the fleshy portion of each chop with a sharp-pointed knife. Lightly fill with stuffing and with a needle and thread make 2 ties.

Remove thread before serving.

Serves 4.

42 ARITAKI MUTTON STEAK

1 lb hogget or young mutton steak
1 clove garlic
1 teaspoon salt
1 teaspoon mustard
1 teaspoon honey

1½ tablespoons cider vinegar
1 tablespoon honey
1 tablespoon cooking oil
2 tablespoons sherry
1-2 tablespoons soured cream

Mix crushed garlic, salt, mustard, honey and vinegar in a flat plate. Trim excess fat from steaks and pound. Place in the marinade and turn to coat them. Marinate mutton not less than 5 hours (hogget 2 hours) turning occasionally. In a heavy-based pan, over moderate heat, melt the honey and oil until lightly brown—it must not burn. Drain steaks and sauté 3 minutes each side in the caramelised honey.

Pour remaining marinade into pan. Spoon sherry over steaks, cover firmly and reduce heat to a low simmer for 10 to 15 minutes. Remove steak and keep warm. Lay a piece of absorbent paper, i.e. paper napkin or brown paper, on the gravy to remove the fat. Boil gravy a minute or so until it is rich brown, thick and syrupy. Reduce heat just below simmering temperature, stir in the soured cream. Check seasoning, replace steaks, spoon gravy over them. Cover firmly and leave hogget steaks about 20 minutes, mutton steaks about 1 hour.
Serves 4.

43 HOGGET STEAK WITH CHINESE GOOSEBERRIES

1 lb hogget steak or leg chops
4 chinese gooseberries
1 tablespoon cooking oil
1 tablespoon butter
1 teaspoon salt
2 tablespoons full cream milk powder

1 tablespoon onion soup powder
pepper—freshly ground
½ cup white wine
2 tablespoons cream
pinch cayenne pepper
parsley

Lay leg chops or steaks (cut ½ inch thick from fillet end of leg) in a flat dish. Peel chinese gooseberries, halve or cut lengthwise in 3 slices. Place on steaks and stand 2 to 3 hours.

Heat butter and oil in pan. Lift off chinese gooseberry slices—sprinkle steaks with salt and rub in mixture of milk and onion soup powder.

Sauté about 15 minutes each side until crisp and golden. Remove, sprinkle with pepper and keep hot. Pour off any fat, sauté chinese gooseberry slices about ½ a minute each side and arrange around the steaks.

Add wine to the pan, scrape up the browning and boil a minute. Reduce heat, stir in the cream and, when hot, add cayenne.

To serve, spoon sauce over the chinese gooseberries and garnish with chopped parsley.
Serves 4.

44 CRUSTY CUTLETS OR STEAKS

6 cutlets—lamb or hogget
parsley
1 small sprig thyme
1 bay leaf
2 tablespoons lemon juice
1 tablespoon peanut oil
2-3 tablespoons butter
3 tablespoons full cream milk powder
1 tablespoon onion soup powder

1 teaspoon honey
1 clove garlic
1½ teaspoons salt
¼ teaspoon pepper—freshly ground
1 large onion
2 apples
2 tablespoons medium-dry white wine
sugar

Pound cutlets or steak to reduce thickness. In a shaker mix the three herbs (bruised) with lemon juice and oil. Over very low heat melt butter in a frying pan—it must not brown. Transfer herbs to melted butter. Soak cutlets in lemon juice and oil—both sides should be well coated. Arrange them in a pile for 30 minutes. Mix to a paste the milk and onion soup powder, melted honey, lemon juice and oil. Season meat with garlic crushed with salt and pepper and spread with paste.

Remove herbs from pan, increase heat and, when butter is sizzling, slightly brown the sliced onion and move it aside. Sauté cutlets each side until they are cooked through, well browned and crisp.

Serve with this apple sauce: peel and grate apples into a small saucepan and add white wine. Stew quickly for about 2 minutes and sweeten to taste.

Serves 6.

45 HOGGET STEAK CHEF D'OEUVRE

Use rump steak sliced across the grain one inch thick

1½ lb hogget steak
vinegar marinade (recipe 208)
1 tablespoon butter
1 tablespoon corn oil
1½ teaspoons salt

freshly ground pepper
1 egg
1 tablespoon mushroom soup powder
3 tablespoons cream or top milk
parsley

Marinate steaks half an hour. Turn once or twice. In a heavy-based pan, heat butter until it starts to brown, add oil and when hot sauté drained steaks 5 minutes each side. Remove, sprinkle with salt and pepper and keep warm.

Beat egg and whisk in the marinade. Put in double boiler (or substitute, glossary), and stir occasionally until it thickens (about 10 minutes). Remove peppercorns.

Pour excess fat from pan, turn heat low and after 1 minute blend the soup powder with the pan browning and stir in the cream. Return steaks to pan, cover and leave about half an hour. Spoon the egg sauce over them and, when thoroughly heated (do not boil), serve garnished with chopped parsley. As one accompaniment, serve sautéed mushrooms.

Serves 6.

46 LAMB RIBLETS SNACKS

Delicious hot or cold for picnics, snack lunches, etc

2 lb riblets
1 onion
2 teaspoons salt
good pinch pepper

1 tablespoon honey
1-2 teaspoons mustard powder
1 clove garlic
1 tablespoon lemon juice

In a heavy-based pan over moderate heat, or electric frying pan, brown the onion and seasoned riblets on all sides. Allow about ½ hour for this. Remove heat and pour off all fat. Paint each riblet with well-mixed baste of honey, mustard, crushed garlic and lemon juice and return to the pan. Cover firmly, reduce heat and simmer gently for about 30 minutes.

Serves 5.

47 HAWKE'S BAY STEAK

3½ lb hogget steak
2 cloves garlic
3½ teaspoons salt
flour
2 tablespoons peanut oil
2 tablespoons butter
2 large onions

1 cup soured cream
3 teaspoons paprika
pinch cayenne
tinfoil
1 cup red wine
parsley
lemon

Remove excess fat from steaks and slice about ¾ inch thick into serving-sized portions.
Season with garlic crushed with salt. Flour well and brown each side in sizzling oil and butter.
Remove and keep warm. Slice and brown onion lightly and spread in bottom of large shallow
baking dish. Arrange steaks on top. Beat soured cream lightly with paprika and cayenne
and pour over steaks. Seal with tinfoil.
Braise in oven at 325° about 45 minutes until tender. Baste occasionally. Lift steaks on to a
serving dish and keep hot. Pour fat from the pan and stir in the wine—boil a few seconds to
dissipate alcohol. Pour this over the steaks and garnish with chopped parsley and lemon
slices.
Serves 14.

48 LAMB OR HOGGET RIBLETS STUFFED

Serve hot or cold

12 riblets
2 teaspoons salt
¼ teaspoon pepper
2 eggs
1 tablespoon milk

3 cups savoury breadcrumbs (recipe 197)
flour
1½ tablespoons butter
1½ tablespoons cooking oil

Trim excess fat from riblets and season with salt and pepper. Use a sharp knife to separate
the meat from the bones, leaving ¼ inch intact at the head of each riblet and ½ inch at the
end.
Beat eggs with milk and lightly mix 1½ tablespoons of this with 1 cup of savoury breadcrumbs.
Open the riblet slits, fill with stuffing, and flatten them a little. Sprinkle with flour. Dip in
beaten egg, and coat with remaining breadcrumb mixture.
Sauté in hot oil and butter until all sides are crisp and nutty brown. Reduce heat a little and
turn occasionally. Allow ¾ to 1 hour total cooking period. Or pre-heat oven to 400°, and
bake about 45 minutes. Turn once when the under surface is nicely browned. When cooked
stand on a rack in the pan for 3 or 4 minutes.
Serves 6.

49 MUTTON CHOPS BAKED WITH MILK

A family favourite

4 mutton loin chops	flour
1¼ teaspoons salt	1 onion
pepper—a generous shake	milk

Season chops and sprinkle with flour. Place surrounded by chopped onion in a flat, shallow baking dish. Pour over sufficient milk almost to cover chops.

Cook in oven pre-heated to 350° for approximately one hour, or until tender. Lift chops from pan and keep warm.

Pour off fat and prepare gravy from richly flavoured base (recipe 170).

Variations: *The milk may be flavoured with one or more of the following: nutmeg, bay leaves, marjoram, parsley, celery, carrots, meat extracts, or soya sauce. A soup powder may replace flour and some of the salt.*

Note: *Sectioned neck, breast, flaps, etc are very successful treated in this way. Bake until the meat is just starting to leave the bone. Prepare a thinnish gravy. Return cooked mutton pieces to this and heat through before serving.*

Serves 4.

Chapter 5

BARBECUES

For satisfactory results it is essential to start the fire approximately 1 to 2 hours before barbecueing. The timing depends upon the depth of embers required to maintain an even heat throughout the cooking period. Cooking should not begin until the flame has died down and the embers are glowing through a thin film of ash.

Charcoal or briquettes are ideal fuel once the fire is established. Both are slow burning, give a fine glow and retain their heat. For even heat, add briquettes to the outer edge of the fire, which should always extend beyond the grilling meat.

The grilling rack or griddle should be moveable, so that it can be raised or lowered as necessary.

Cut meat in serving-size pieces and season with 1 teaspoon salt per lb unless using a highly seasoned basting sauce. Serve all barbecued meats without delay. Mutton should first be marinated (Chapter 18).

Barbecue thick cuts (1 to $1\frac{1}{4}$ inches) approximately 8 inches from embers. Lower rack accordingly, i.e. flattened cutlets or steaks (about $\frac{1}{2}$ inch thick) will barbecue quickly 3 or 4 inches from hot coals. Turn all portions once with long-handled tongs or fork the moment they are browned to the desired degree.

When using a basting sauce, heat it, and with a long-handled spoon, baste meats frequently while barbecueing. Alternatively, quickly dip chops, etc into the hot sauce, shake well and return to grill.

Vegetables: Root vegetables, or onions, peeled or unpeeled, pumpkin or marrow unpeeled. Wash and prepare beforehand. See Chapter 19. Season and top each piece with a small knob of butter. Parcel singly in double thicknesses of tinfoil. Seal and arrange in and around the hot embers. Turn at intervals and allow about half the time required for roasting. Use a fork to test when cooked.

To cook buttered peas or any quick cooking green vegetable, put saucepan on grilling rack fairly close to embers.

Foods to be associated on a skewer should be cut to much the same size and require a similar grilling period. Foods which require a prolonged cooking period should be pre-cooked until almost tender.

Cut meat to be skewered across the grain, usually into one inch cubes. Sprinkle with salt before barbecueing and, before quickly serving, sprinkle generously with freshly ground black pepper.

Here are some excellent basic barbecue sauces.

50 JEAN'S BARBECUE SAUCE

½ pint tomato sauce
2 oz olive oil
2 dessertspoons soya sauce
good pinch paprika
good pinch curry powder
good pinch ground allspice
1 teaspoon ground ginger

1 dessertspoon tarragon vinegar or
use wine or cider vinegar and a
teaspoon dried tarragon
1 level teaspoon prepared mustard or
mix 1½ teaspoons mustard powder with
soya sauce
1 clove crushed garlic

Agitate vigorously to combine. Store in screw-top bottle and, if possible, stand 2 or 3 days. Shake well before using. Mixture will keep several weeks.

51 AMERICAN BASTING SAUCE OR MARINADE

1 tablespoon honey
1 teaspoon mustard
2 tablespoons vinegar
1 small onion grated
1 rib celery grated
1 clove garlic crushed with salt

1 teaspoon salt
good shake fresh pepper
pinch of cayenne or chilli powder
½ cup tomato sauce
¼ cup water
1 teaspoon Worcester sauce

Dissolve honey and mustard in warmed vinegar. Beat well with other ingredients and allow to infuse about one hour. Boil and use while still warm as a baste or marinade.
Suitable as an accompanying sauce.

52 ARGENTINE BASTE

Keeps indefinitely. Prepare at least a fortnight before required.
Quarter fill a 26 oz bottle with common salt, add about 10 cloves mashed garlic and 4 dried chillies, or a bare teaspoon of chilli powder. Fill bottle almost to capacity with cold water and seal with screw top. Agitate well at frequent intervals until salt dissolves. To baste—pierce a small hole in bottle top and baste meats generously while grilling. Do not use any other seasoning or sauces.

53 BARBECUED LOIN CHOPS A L'INDIENNE

Use either thick loin chops, twin cutlets (two as one) from best end neck or thick steaks. Slit fleshy eye of each chop, etc to form pocket. Sprinkle with salt and insert ½ teaspoon of curry powder and ½ teaspoon finely chopped onion in each. Baste with apple-juice marinade (recipe 210) minus cloves and grill until the fatty tissue is well browned. Turn and repeat. Sprinkle with pepper before serving.

54 HAWAIIAN LOIN CHOPS

Use either thick loin chops, twin cutlets (two as one) from best end neck or thick steaks. Sprinkle with salt and pepper. Slit fleshy eye of each chop etc to form pocket. Insert mixture of $\frac{1}{2}$ teaspoon mustard and $\frac{1}{2}$ teaspoon vinegar into each pocket. Add $\frac{1}{2}$ teaspoon well chopped or crushed canned pineapple and a pinch of salt. A little minced bacon may also be added. Concoct fillings to suit occasion. Grill until the fatty tissue is browned and just crisp. Half minute before turning lightly paint grilled side with mixture of melted butter and honey. Repeat second side before serving.

For further recipes see Grills, Chapter 4.

SKEWER COOKING:

The following combinations will serve as a guide.

55 MUTTON OR HOGGET AND SOYA SHISH KEBABS

Mutton steaks
Soya sauce marinade (recipe 206)

small green onions or shallots
thin bacon rashers

Pound steaks, cut into one inch cubes and marinate up to 5 hours.

Place drained cubes and onions alternately on the skewer, with cubes of meat at each end. Weave strips of bacon round the onions and grill about 8 inches from heat. Turn frequently. Allow 20 minutes if preferred well cooked. Basting is optional.

56 SHISH KEBABS WITH AUBERGINE

2 lb lean lamb
aubergine
small onions
small'firm tomatoes
small mushrooms

green peppers
2 teaspoons salt
melted butter
freshly ground pepper

Cut lamb into one inch cubes. Peel and cube aubergine, slice onion, halve tomatoes, mushrooms whole or cut to size. Remove veins and seed from green peppers, and cut to size. Season and alternate ingredients on skewers, with a cube of aubergine at each end. Sandwich together. Grill on rack about 3 inches from hot coals. Turn frequently and, with a brush, baste lightly and often with melted butter. Sprinkle with pepper. Allow about 2 minutes each side.

57 SHISH KEBABS WITH PINEAPPLE

Thin strips lean lamb
pineapple cubes
bacon
stoned olives

salt
pineapple juice marinade (recipe 211)
butter
pepper—freshly ground

Prepare marinade as baste. Alternate pineapple, bacon cut to same size and halved olives on skewer. Sprinkle 1 teaspoon salt over 1 lb lamb strips and weave them in form of a plait round pineapple etc. Grill on rack about 4 inches from coals. Turn frequently. Baste several times with a brush, alternating marinade and melted butter.

Note: Pineapple may be replaced by cooked prunes, canned apricots or peaches, halved and quartered, bananas in one-inch lengths or cubed apple. (Use a variety which remains whole when cooked).

58 SHISH KEBABS WITH LAMB'S FRY

Lamb's fry
small mushrooms
salt

bacon squares
melted butter
pepper

Cut fry in one-inch cubes and peel mushrooms—cut to size if large. Sprinkle both with salt (1 teaspoon per lb of fry). Alternate on skewers with bacon squares.

Grill on rack about 3 inches from hot coals for 4 to 5 minutes. Turn frequently, basting with melted butter. Sprinkle with pepper before serving.

59 KIDNEY SHISH KEBABS

Sheep's kidneys
bacon rashers
mushrooms
salt

pepper
pinch marjoram
butter

Slice kidneys, bacon and mushrooms to same size and thickness.

Lightly season kidneys and mushrooms. Thread on skewers in following order—bacon, kidney, bacon, mushrooms, bacon, kidney, etc.

Paint generously with melted butter and place on grilling rack 2 to 3 inches from heat and rotate 2 to 3 minutes to brown evenly. Be careful not to overcook. Serve immediately on skewers.

Chapter 6

TO PAN-BRAISE OR CASSEROLE LAMB, HOGGET AND MUTTON

These methods are recommended for the cooking of mutton and the less tender cuts of hogget, scrag end neck, middle neck chops, spanish neck, breast or shanks. In fact use any parts of the carcase, with or without bone, and cut to suitable sizes (ie for stews, curries etc about 1 to $1\frac{1}{4}$ inch cubes).

Tender cuts require only a short cooking period although the flavour of the stock is usually so good it can be rewarding to reduce the temperature and prolong the cooking period. After the initial preparation very little attention is needed before serving. Meats may even be cooked the previous day and slowly reheated to boiling point before serving.

An electric frying pan is the ideal cooking utensil; or, use either a heavy-based pan with a tight lid, or a covered casserole, and braise on top of stove or in oven.

60 BASIC BRAISING RECIPE

meat	flour
salt	soup powder (optional)
pepper	cooking oil or fat
garlic	1 large onion
a compatible herb	

Trim excess fat from meat, and cut to the required size and thickness. Season each pound with 1 teaspoon salt, a generous shake of pepper, $\frac{1}{2}$ to 1 clove garlic (chop and crush with salt). A herb or herbs may be mixed with the seasoning.

Sprinkle with 1 tablespoon of flour and/or 1 tablespoon of soup powder.

Smear the pan with either butter, cooking oil or fat. Heat and slightly sauté some chopped seasoned onion. Remove and keep hot. Brown seasoned meat (if using curry stock see recipe 64), pour off fat, and return onion to pan. Pour in some hot stock (recipes 61 to 64) to just cover base of pan. Heat to boiling point. Reduce to a slow simmer, check seasoning and cover firmly. Before serving, to simplify and hasten the skimming of fat, tilt pan as high as contents will allow, support the 1 or 2 legs and leave 2 or 3 minutes until fat drains to one spot. Pour off and gather up residue with a paper napkin.

Approximate timing:

Lamb steaks and tender cuts—10 to 30 minutes, according to thickness.
Lamb neck, breast and shanks—$1\frac{1}{4}$ to $1\frac{3}{4}$ hours.
Hogget tender cuts—20 to 40 minutes.
Hogget neck, breast and shanks—$2\frac{1}{2}$ to $2\frac{3}{4}$ hours.
Mutton tender cuts—$1\frac{1}{2}$ to 2 hours.
Mutton neck, breast and shanks—3 to $3\frac{1}{2}$ hours.

61 FRUIT STOCK

Choose from the following fruit:

(a) *canned fruit :*

pineapple (rounds, cubed or grated)
peaches (sliced)
apricots (sliced)

the syrup as stock
lemon juice or cider vinegar
to counteract sweetness

(b) *fresh fruits:*

(i) *After the fat has been removed grate 1 or 2 tart apples over the browned meat and sprinkle lightly with sugar or slice cored apples in rings and use a little canned apple juice flavoured to taste.*

(ii) *Chinese Gooseberries: Peel thinly. Slice and sprinkle with sugar. Stand $\frac{3}{4}$ hour. Treat as canned fruit.*

62 CANNED PINEAPPLE STOCK

1 12 oz can pineapple
1 green pepper (optional)
1 teaspoon mustard powder
2 tablespoons cider vinegar

1 tablespoon chopped mint
cream
pepper—freshly ground

Strain juice from pineapple. Halve sufficient rings, cubes or pieces to cover the browned meat generously. Remove seeds and veins from green pepper, shred and sprinkle it over pineapple. Mix mustard with vinegar and stir into pineapple juice. Heat, stir in mint and pour over the pan contents. Add a little cream after removing fat. Reheat and sprinkle with pepper before serving.

Peaches and apricots: *Treat similarly. Increase the cider vinegar if necessary.*

63 STOCK FROM LEFTOVER GRAVY WITH VEGETABLES

1 tablespoon butter
1 cup chopped vegetables
salt
pepper
1$\frac{1}{2}$ cups tasty gravy or stock

sugar
$\frac{1}{4}$ teaspoon mixed herbs
2 tablespoons mint sauce, or
  1 tablespoon cider vinegar and
  1 teaspoon sugar

In a heavy-based saucepan heat butter,until sizzling.Add vegetables, i.e. some of the following: leek, tomato, celery, marrow, onion, parsley, young green beans, peas, cauliflower or a packet of frozen mixed vegetables thawed. Season with a pinch of salt, pepper and sugar. Reduce heat, cover and simmer slowly for 5 minutes. Add remaining ingredients and when simmering, pour over the browned meat and onion.

64 CURRY STOCK

Over 1 lb meat browning in pan sprinkle 2
   teaspoons curry powder (or to taste)
1 apple
1 teaspoon sugar
To 1½ cups of stock or water add:
2½ teaspoons soya sauce

1½ teaspoons vinegar
small piece of green ginger root crushed
   and chopped
½ teaspoon coriander
1 rib celery shredded
pinch chilli powder

*Grate raw apple over browned meat and sprinkle with sugar. Heat stock mixture and gently
pour sufficient hot stock into pan to not quite cover meat. (Do not dislodge apple.) Serve
with boiled rice.*

65 MUSHROOM STOCK

Served with lamb or hogget steaks or cutlets

½ lb mushrooms
2 tablespoons butter
pinch marjoram
1 shallot or spring onion with
   green top
1 packet mushroom soup powder

paprika
pinch salt
1 cup cold water
¾ cup milk
2 tablespoons cream

*Wipe mushroom tops and stalks with a damp cloth before slicing them. Heat butter in small,
heavy-based saucepan. When sizzling hot add marjoram, mushrooms, shredded onion,
pinch paprika and salt. Cover and simmer very slowly 3 minutes. Stir in soup powder mixed
with water and milk until it thickens. When simmering remove from heat and stir in cream.
Pour over browned meat etc. Serve sprinkled with paprika.*
*Field mushrooms : Discard stalk ends. Peel mushrooms. Put peelings and stalks in colander
and wash thoroughly under running water. Put in saucepan, add ½ teaspoon salt, just cover
with cold water and simmer (covered) 20 minutes. Strain and press peels against strainer to
collect all juice. Use this instead of salt and water. If omitting all milk add an extra tablespoon
of cream.*

66 LAGER BEER OR CIDER STOCK

1 teaspoon mustard powder
1 cup beer or cider
1 or 2 apples

brown sugar
cream

*Mix mustard with a little beer or cider, add the remainder, bring to boil and pour into pan.
Grate a generous coating of apple over the browned meat and sprinkle with sugar, 1 teaspoon
per apple. After removing any fat a few minutes before serving, add 2 tablespoons of cream
into the gravy and check seasoning.*
*Note: Grated canned pineapple with a little juice may replace apple, but in this case omit
sugar.*

67 BACHELOR'S DELIGHT

leg or chump chops
cooking oil
onion
salt
pepper

flour
1 cup lager or light beer
1 tablespoon full cream milk powder
a little lemon juice

Remove practically all fat from chops (they may be boned). Smear pan base with oil and heat to 250°. Place thin onion slices in pan. Sprinkle meat with salt (1 teaspoon per pound), freshly ground pepper and flour. Place on top of the onion and cover pan. Close vent.

After half an hour turn chops. (They should not brown.) Pour over 1 large breakfast cup of lager beer and replace lid firmly. Simmer another half hour. Mix milk powder to a paste with lemon juice.Thin with a little pan gravy and stir to blend. Reduce heat to 200°, cover and leave another half hour. Mutton chops 1½ hours.

68 AUSTRALIAN LAMB WITH SPAGHETTI

1 lb lean lamb
peanut oil
salt
2 large onions chopped
1 clove garlic crushed
1 large carrot cubed
1 rasher bacon chopped
pepper—freshly ground

1 green pepper—seeded and shredded
2 tablespoons chopped parsley
1 cup tomato puree or juice
2 teaspoons soya sauce
1 tablespoon Worcester sauce
½ cup shredded celery
¼ teaspoon sugar
cheese

Cut lamb into ½ inch cubes.

Heat a bare tablespoon of oil, add ½ teaspoon salt and lightly brown onions and garlic. After approximately 2 minutes add carrot and bacon. Lift from pan and brown meat. Return sautéed vegetables and all other ingredients with 1 teaspoon salt and a generous shake of pepper. Simmer very slowly for 1 hour or until cooked. Mixture should be juicy but not watery.

Serve on a bed of spaghetti or noodles. Top with grated parmesan or any other mature cheese.

Serves 4.

69 FRICASSEE OF MUTTON, HOGGET OR LAMB

For this economical family meal any cuts may be used, but scrag end neck, neck chops, breast and flaps are delicious.

Allow per lb of mutton, hogget or lamb:

1 teaspoon salt
generous shake of pepper

1 large onion
parsley sauce supreme (recipe 179)

Cut meat into serving-size pieces—about ½ inch thick—and season. Place each piece in contact with the base of the frying pan set at 200°. Cover with sliced onion. Put lid on pan and turn meat halfway through cooking period. There should be no evidence of browning. Sweat spring lamb pieces 2 to 3 hours; hogget pieces 3 to 4 hours; mutton 5 to 6 hours, or until tender.

Prepare parsley sauce supreme. Before placing meat in sauce, lightly scrape each piece across the pan edge to remove any clinging fat.

Pour pan liquor into a bowl and stand this in cold water. Lift off the fat. Heat the liquor and stir into the fricassee.

To mingle these delicate flavours, transfer to a double boiler. Alternatively simmer very slowly half an hour, or until required.

70 CANTERBURY LEG CHOPS

1 leg chop per serving
Allow per lb:

cooking oil
1 teaspoon salt

$\frac{1}{2}$ cup mint sauce (recipe 181)
2 tablespoons chutney

Smear pan with oil. When hot, sauté seasoned chops each side until fatty tissue is nut-brown. Place in casserole, and pour over mixture of mint sauce and chutney. Cover firmly. Bake at 300°.
Allow hogget chops 1$\frac{1}{4}$ to 1$\frac{1}{2}$ hours until tender. Sprinkle with freshly ground pepper.
Note: *Marinate mutton chops in mint sauce and chutney for about 5 hours. Drain, season and proceed as above. Increase the cooking period to 2$\frac{1}{4}$ to 2$\frac{3}{4}$ hours.*

71 SOUTHLAND MUTTON STEAKS

Also suitable for neck chops and riblets

1$\frac{1}{2}$ lb steak
1$\frac{1}{2}$ teaspoons salt
$\frac{1}{4}$ teaspoon baking soda
pepper

cooking oil
2 tablespoons cider vinegar
parsley

Mix salt and baking soda well with a good shake of pepper. Rub this into trimmed serving-size steaks or chops and stand about two hours. Sauté each side in hot oil. Sprinkle with vinegar. Reduce heat and cover firmly. Simmer slowly 1$\frac{1}{2}$ to 2$\frac{1}{2}$ hours until tender. Pour off all fat. Garnish with chopped parsley.
Note: *An equal amount of canned fruit juice (eg pineapple, apricot, apple or peach) may be mixed with the cider vinegar.*
Serves 6, or 1 chop per serving.

72 FRUITY FARE

Mutton, hogget or lamb riblets and flaps braised

2 lb breast of hogget
2 teaspoons salt
$\frac{1}{4}$ teaspoon pepper
$\frac{1}{2}$ teaspoon dried marjoram
3 tablespoons flour
bacon or mutton fat
1 large onion

2 tablespoons cider vinegar
1 small can pineapple
1 small can peas
1$\frac{1}{2}$ cups tomato purée
pepper
2 tablespoons chopped mint

Cut breast riblets and trimmed flaps into oblongs about 1 by 2 inches, and coat with mixture of salt, pepper, marjoram and flour. Smear pan with a little fat. When very hot, brown meat and sliced onion. Stir in cider vinegar, pineapple juice, liquor from peas, tomato purée, and a generous grinding of black pepper.
Cover pan firmly and simmer, or bake slowly (250°) in a covered casserole 1$\frac{3}{4}$ hours. Skim off any fat. Add pineapple, peas and mint, and simmer another 15 to 30 minutes until tender.
Allow mutton riblets approximately 2$\frac{3}{4}$ hours.
For spring lamb riblets and flaps use lemon juice instead of cider vinegar. Bake 1$\frac{1}{4}$ to 1$\frac{1}{2}$ hours or until tender.
Serves 8.

73 CHOPS WITH APPLE JUICE

Use lamb, hogget or mutton chops or steak

4 chops
1 clove garlic
1 teaspoon salt
pepper
bacon fat or butter
1 large onion
1 teaspoon crushed green ginger root
1 teaspoon sugar

1 tablespoon flour or
  1½ tablespoons pea and ham
  soup powder
1 cup canned apple juice
1 tablespoon lemon juice
1 teaspoon lemon rind
1 large apple
cream

Trim fat from chops. Rub all over with garlic crushed with salt and pepper. Sprinkle with a little flour. Heat some bacon fat or butter until sizzling hot. Brown the lightly seasoned sliced onion and put in a casserole. Brown the seasoned chops or steak and place on top of onion. Pour off most of the fat. Add well crushed ginger. Blend in sugar and flour or the soup powder, and scrape up all the brown bits from the pan. Stir in apple juice, half the lemon juice and rind. Let sauce boil, and pour over chops.Top these with grated apple. Sprinkle with sugar, the remaining lemon juice and rind.Cover firmly and cook at 275° in oven.

Allow lamb chops about 1 hour ; hogget 1½ to 2 hours, and mutton about 3 hours. Before serving skim off any fat.

Add about 1 tablespoon cream or to taste. Check seasoning and re-heat.

Note: *Preserved peaches, pineapple or apricots are suitable substitutes for apple. Cider vinegar may be added to taste instead of lemon juice .*

Serves 4.

74 TOMATO AND CORN CASSEROLE

7 stewing chops (mutton, hogget or lamb)
1 clove garlic
2 teaspoons salt
¼ teaspoon pepper
2 tablespoons butter
1 medium onion
2 ribs celery
2 tablespoons shredded green pepper

1 cup tomato juice
1 teaspoon sugar
½ teaspoon basil
1 can whole kernel corn
1 packet onion soup powder
1 teaspoon paprika
½ cup top milk
1 cup grated cheese

Pre-heat oven to 375°.

Rub chops with crushed garlic, salt and pepper. Brown in a covered dish in the oven. Allow lamb chops 40 minutes, hogget 50 minutes, mutton 1¼ hours. Turn once.

In a heavy-based saucepan heat 2 tablespoons butter. Add lightly seasoned chopped onion, shredded celery and green pepper. Reduce heat, cover and simmer gently for about 5 minutes—do not brown.

Add mixture of tomato juice, sugar and basil. Then add corn and liquor and allow to boil. Blend thickening of soup powder, paprika, top milk and grated cheese. Stir in the thickening until sauce simmers and keep warm.

When chops are nicely brown, pour off all fat. Pour over the corn sauce and top with grated cheese. Return uncovered to 350° oven for 40 to 45 minutes.

Serves 7.

75 WAIKATO CHOPS
Mutton chops with beer and cabbage

6 mutton chops	1 medium onion
2 teaspoons salt	1 clove garlic
pepper	½ teaspoon white sugar
1 lemon	caraway seeds (optional)
1 tablespoon cooking oil	½ teaspoon mustard powder
butter	1 cup beer
cabbage	1 dessertspoon brown sugar
1 cooking apple	½ teaspoon cinnamon

Trim fat from chops and sprinkle each side with 1½ teaspoons salt, pepper and a squeeze of lemon juice. Heat oil and 1 tablespoon butter and quickly brown chops. Shred 3 cups cabbage and mix with grated apple, chopped onion and crushed garlic. Sprinkle with ½ teaspoon salt, some pepper, the sugar and a few caraway seeds. Lift to distribute. Butter casserole and put in a layer of the cabbage mixture. Place chops on top and sprinkle with half a teaspoon grated lemon rind. Repeat these layers. Cover with cabbage mixture, and a squeeze of lemon juice. Mix mustard with a little of the beer, stir in the rest and pour into casserole. Sprinkle with brown sugar and cinnamon. Dot with butter and put lid on firmly. Bake in oven at 300° for 2½ to 3 hours, depending on thickness of chops.
Alternatively, this dish may be simmered on top of the stove over low heat, in which case saucepan should occasionally be shaken gently during cooking.
Serves 6.

76 GOLFER'S CASSEROLE

6 mutton chops	¼ teaspoon mixed herbs
1½ teaspoons salt	1 large onion
½ teaspoon pepper	
Sauce :	
1 tablespoon fat	1 teaspoon sugar
1 rib celery	1 packet pea and ham soup powder
1 carrot	1 medium-sized can tomato juice
½ apple	Worcester sauce
pinch salt	red pepper sauce

Pre-heat oven to 200° for a 5 to 6 hour cooking period, or, 180° for 8 hours.
Trim most of the fat from chops and sprinkle with seasoning. Put sliced onion in casserole, add chops and 1 cup water. Cover firmly. Half fill a pan with water and place it about the middle of the oven. Stand casserole in this.
When required, pour liquor from casserole into a bowl and stand in cold water to set fat. Return covered casserole to oven. Turn off heat.
Sauce:
Heat 1 tablespoon fat (from liquor) until sizzling. Mix in finely chopped vegetables, grated apple, salt and sugar. Mix soup powder with tomato juice and fat-free liquor. Add and stir until it boils and simmer 10 minutes. Add a dash of Worcester and red pepper sauces and pour over meat. Cover and heat casserole slowly on top of the stove until it boils.
Alternative: Vegetable sauce (recipe 178).
Serves 6.

77 HAVELOCK MUTTON CHOPS

Simple to prepare

4 mutton chops	1 large onion
2 teaspoons salt	2 tablespoons tomato sauce
pepper	1 tablespoon Worcester or soya sauce
1 teaspoon sugar	boiling water
2 tablespoons flour	

Trim most of the fat from chops. Season with mixture of salt, pepper, sugar and flour. Place on sliced onion in casserole. Include other chopped vegetables if you wish. Put tomato and Worcester sauce in breakfast cup and fill with boiling water. Stir and pour over chops. Heat oven to 300°. Place lid firmly on casserole and bake 2½ hours or longer until tender. Before serving pour off any fat. Collect residue with paper napkin.
This dish may be slowly simmered on top of stove.
Serves 4.

78 HAVELOCK CASSEROLE

4 mutton chops	1 cup stock
2 teaspoons salt	1 tablespoon cider vinegar
pepper	2 teaspoons sugar
1 large onion	1 tablespoon flour

Trim excess fat from chops and season with salt and pepper. Place on sliced onion in casserole, and cover firmly. Heat oven to 400° and bake chops until they are nicely brown (¾ to 1 hour).
Pour off fat. Add 1 cup hot stock, 1 tablespoon cider vinegar and 2 teaspoons sugar. Return covered casserole to oven and bring to boil. Stir in thickening (see Glossary). After 15 minutes reduce heat to 250° and bake another 45 minutes or until tender.
Alternatives: *Add chopped vegetables, garlic, herbs, etc to stock. Use soup powder as thickening.*
Serves 4.

79 RED WINE HOGGET CASSEROLE

3 lb middle neck chops	½ pint red wine
2 tablespoons butter or cooking oil	½ pint hot water
1 large onion	4 tablespoons tomato juice or purée
4 medium cloves garlic	¼ teaspoon marjoram or oreganum
3-3½ teaspoons salt	2-3 tablespoons parsley
	¼ cup cream

Heat butter in frying pan until it starts to brown. Add sliced onion and chops seasoned with garlic crushed with salt. Brown lightly. Add half the wine and water. Cook 5 minutes. Put in casserole, cover and cook in oven pre-heated to 300° for about ½ hour. Add tomato juice, marjoram and chopped parsley. Continue cooking until meat is tender, approximately 2 hours. About 10 minutes before serving, lift meat from casserole and keep warm. Pour off all fat. Stir in remaining wine and hot water. Replace meat, cover and reheat until it reaches boiling point. Blend in the cream. When thoroughly heated serve with boiled rice or buttered potatoes, and garnish with chopped parsley.
Serves 10.

80 MUTTON CHOPS WITH SWEET POTATOES

6 mutton chops
2½ teaspoons salt
¼ teaspoon pepper
cooking oil
8 medium-size sweet potatoes
2 tablespoons brown sugar

3 tablespoons butter
2 tablespoons cider
½ teaspoon nutmeg
4 onions
1 or 2 rashers lean bacon
3 apples

Trim fat from chops, pound to reduce thickness, and season with 2 teaspoons salt and a good shake pepper. Brown each side in a little hot oil. Boil or steam sweet potatoes. Peel and beat with 1 tablespoon brown sugar, the melted butter, cider and nutmeg until smooth and creamy. Season to taste. In a buttered casserole arrange layers in the following order: sliced onions, sweet potatoes, chops, diced bacon, grated apples, sliced onions, etc. Finally top with a layer of sweet potatoes and sprinkle with remaining brown sugar. Dot generously with butter and bake in oven at 325° for 2½ hours.
Serves 6.

81 CASSEROLED MUTTON SHANKS

4 shanks
1 large onion
2 teaspoons salt
pepper
1½ tablespoons flour
½ teaspoon sugar

1 carrot
3 ribs celery
½ cup tomato pulp
1 tablespoon Worcester sauce
1½ cups cold water

Arrange a layer of sliced onion on the bottom of the casserole. Put shanks on top. Mix salt, pepper, flour, and sugar and sprinkle on meat and onion. Cover with sliced carrot and celery. Pour in mixture of tomato pulp, sauce and water.
Cover and bake at 300° for 3 to 3½ hours until tender.
Serves 4.

82 HOGGET SHANK STEW

4 hogget shanks
1½ teaspoons salt
½ teaspoon sugar
¼ teaspoon pepper
¼ teaspoon mixed herbs

1 large onion
water or stock
1 tablespoon pearl barley
1 large carrot
1½ to 2 tablespoons flour

Put shanks, seasoning and chopped onion in a wide saucepan. Cover with water or stock, and bring to boil. Add barley, reduce heat, cover firmly and simmer slowly about 2 hours. Add diced carrot and other vegetables of your choice. Simmer ½ hour. Mix flour with cold water to about the consistency of cream and stir into the remaining liquor until it thickens. Simmer 15 minutes before serving.
Serves 4.

83 HONG KONG CASSEROLE

1½ lb lean hogget or lamb steaks
4 tablespoons butter
salt
1 large onion
¼ lb mushrooms
2 cups cold boiled rice
1 tablespoon pea and ham soup powder
1 clove garlic
a generous pinch pepper

cornflour
2 teaspoons soya sauce (or to taste)
1½ cups warm stock or milk and water
½ cup breadcrumbs
1 cup cheese
2 tablespoons chopped parsley
pinch cayenne
½ teaspoon nutmeg

Heat 3 tablespoons butter in casserole until sizzling hot. Sprinkle ½ teaspoon salt over sliced onions and mushrooms and lightly sauté a few minutes. Add cold boiled rice. Sprinkle with soup powder and stir well.
Slice meat ¼ inch thick. Season with garlic, chopped and crushed with 1½ teaspoons salt and a shake of pepper. Coat with cornflour. Heat remaining butter in a pan and sauté until nicely browned. Arrange on prepared rice, include pan drippings and sprinkle with soya sauce. Pour over stock and top with the mixture of breadcrumbs, grated cheese, chopped parsley, cayenne and nutmeg, spread evenly. Place in centre of oven and bake for approximately 1½ hours at 325˚. Topping should be crisp and golden.
Serves 6.

84 STEAMED SOUP-POWDER STEW

2 lb of any mutton or hogget pieces
½ teaspoon salt
good shake pepper

1 teaspoon sugar
½ packet of each of the following soup
    powders—onion, tomato, pea and ham

In a bowl, place 1 to 1¼ inch cubes (or size to suit joint) mutton, trimmed of excess fat and seasoned. Coat well with soup powders. Place uncovered bowl in saucepan containing sufficient boiling water to reach halfway up the bowl. Place firm lid on saucepan and keep water boiling 2½ hours (replenishing when necessary) or until meat is very tender. Pour off fat. Sprinkle with parsley and serve with vegetables.
Serves 8.
Variations: To the above ingredients add: ½ cup chopped prunes and 3 tablespoons red wine: or ½ cup chopped dried apricots or peaches, 1 teaspoon mustard, pinch of nutmeg, pinch of chilli powder, a little garlic, 3 tablespoons beer.

85 SHANKS IN CAPER SAUCE

6 shanks (mutton, hogget or lamb)
1½ teaspoons salt
freshly ground pepper

1 large onion
caper sauce (recipe 172)

Season shanks and lay in frying pan. Top with sliced onion, cover firmly and cook lamb 3 to 3½ hours at 200˚, or until tender. Do not brown. Skim fat from pan juice and stir juice into caper sauce. Pour over shanks, cover and serve when thoroughly heated.
Allow hogget shanks 4½ hours; mutton shanks 5½ hours or longer.
Serves 6.

86 PICNIC SHANKS

For each shank allow:
½ teaspoon honey
¼ teaspoon mustard
½ clove garlic
2 teaspoons cider vinegar or
2 teaspoons lemon juice for lamb shanks

½ teaspoon salt
freshly ground pepper
tinfoil

Mix honey, mustard, mashed garlic and cider vinegar. Paint shanks with mixture and lay meaty portions in remaining liquor for approximately 1 hour. Turn several times. Sprinkle with salt and pepper and completely seal in tinfoil. Place shanks in roasting pan or frying pan so they do not touch.
Bake in oven at 300°. Allow lamb shanks 1½ to 1¾ hours ; hogget 2½ hours ; mutton approximately 3 hours.
In frying pan (covered) cook at 250° for 2½ to 3½ hours.
Unwrap parcels when quite cold.Serve in lettuce leaves with hard-boiled eggs halved,wedges of tomato and thick unpeeled cucumber slices. Sprinkle with parsley.
For a complete hot meal: *Prepare shanks as above and place on tinfoil. Add a little chopped onion, parsley, celery, diced carrot, tomato, sliced green beans and diced potatoes. Season with a pinch of salt and add a teaspoon of butter. Seal foil. Cook as above. Open carefully. Skim off any fat before serving.*

87 QUEENSLAND RAGOUT

Use scrag end neck, breasts, flaps or shoulder chops.

2 lb mutton shoulder chops
2 teaspoons salt
¼ teaspoon pepper
2 teaspoons cooking oil
2 large onions
1 packet pea and ham soup powder
2 cups hot water
1 tablespoon soya sauce

2 tablespoons butter
1 rib celery with green top
1 inner green leek top shredded
2 tablespoons chopped parsley
3 large tomatoes
1 teaspoon dried basil
1 teaspoon sugar
seasoning
1 lb young green beans

Remove excess fat from chops or serving size pieces and sprinkle with salt and pepper.
Smear pan with oil. When moderately hot, add meat and 1 sliced onion. Brown one side, turn. Top chops with onion and when brown underneath remove and keep hot. Pour all fat from pan. Add soup powder (mix first with a little of the water), water and soya sauce. Stir well. Return meat, cover and simmer slowly for about 2½ hours. Skim off any fat.
In a small saucepan heat butter until sizzling. Add the onion finely chopped, shredded celery and leek top, chopped parsley, skinned and sliced tomatoes, basil, sugar, ¼ teaspoon salt and a good shake of pepper. Cover firmly and simmer very slowly 5 minutes. Take care not to brown. Stir in finely sliced beans and combine with meat. Cover and simmer slowly or cook in oven at 250° until chops are tender—about ½ to ¾ hour. Serve with a puree of potatoes. Sprinkle with chopped parsley.
Serves 8.

88 WAIREKE MUTTON STEW

A firm winter favourite

Use scrag end or middle neck, breast, flaps or mutton chops.

1½ lb any hogget or mutton	freshly ground pepper
1 large onion	1 teaspoon sugar
1 large carrot	½ teaspoon mixed herbs
1 rib celery with green top	2 tablespoons flour
1½ teaspoons salt	

Remove excess fat and cut meat with or without bone into pieces about 1½ inches square or to suit specific joint. Place on piece of paper and mix with chopped vegetables. Sprinkle with mixture of salt, pepper, sugar and herbs. Coat with flour. Place in deep bowl (without lid) which will fit inside a saucepan containing sufficient boiling water to come halfway up the bowl. Put firm lid on saucepan and keep water boiling (replenish when necessary) for 2½ to 3 hours. Meat must be very tender. Although no liquid is added to the bowl, when the meat is cooked it will be filled with a delicious gravy. Pour fat from bowl. Lift off residue with paper napkin or ice cube before serving with vegetables.
Serves 4 to 5.

89 DOMINION GOULASH

Neck and breast of mutton with beer. Any mutton pieces are suitable.

2 lb neck and breast	2 carrots
2 teaspoons salt	2 ribs celery
¼ teaspoon pepper	1 leek top (inner leaves)
1 teaspoon mustard powder	1 apple
¼ teaspoon nutmeg	3 parsley branches
1 dessertspoon honey	sprig of rosemary
1 tablespoon cooking oil or butter	2 bay leaves or 1 teaspoon mixed herbs
2 large onions	½ pint beer
1 clove garlic	2 teaspoons soya sauce
2 tablespoons flour	stock or water
2 rashers bacon	½ cup soured cream

Remove excess fat from meat. To cut up, see recipe above. Season with mixture of salt, pepper, mustard and nutmeg. Smear with honey (warm it in cold weather). Stand about one hour. Heat oil in heavy-based saucepan and lightly brown the sliced onions and crushed garlic. Remove and keep hot. Flour meat, brown in saucepan and return onion and garlic. Add bacon, carrots, celery, leek, and apple, all finely chopped. Add parsley, rosemary and bay leaves tied into bouquet garni. Pour over beer and soya sauce with just sufficient stock or water to cover the ingredients.
Bring to boil, reduce heat, cover firmly and simmer slowly until the meat is just starting to separate from bones (3 to 3½ hours). Goulash may also be cooked in a casserole in oven at 275°.
Remove bouquet of herbs and skim off all fat. If some thickening is required, stir in up to ½ cup of soured cream (or make substitute with 3 tablespoons full cream milk powder mixed with a little lemon juice). Reheat before serving.
Alternatively, use 1-2 tablespoons flour with water as thickening. Stir into the goulash until the gravy thickens. Simmer another 10 to 15 minutes before serving with vegetables.
Variation: *Use cider instead of beer. Quite a different flavour, and very good, too.*
Serves 8.

90 QUEENSTOWN CASSEROLE

2 lb scrag end, middle neck and/or
   flaps of mutton, hogget or lamb
1 clove garlic
2 teaspoons salt
⅛ teaspoon pepper
4 tablespoons cider vinegar
1 tablespoon honey
2 teaspoons mustard
2 large onions

2 tablespoons bacon fat
3 tablespoons flour
1 large carrot
1 rib celery with green top
½ cup tomato sauce
3 tablespoons Worcester or soya sauce
2 cups hot water
parsley

*Remove excess fat and cut meat into neat pieces. Mix marinade of crushed garlic, salt,
pepper, vinegar, honey and mustard. Marinate meat—up to 2 hours, stirring occasionally.
Brown sliced onions lightly in hot fat. Place in casserole and keep warm. Lift meat from
marinade, flour evenly and brown. Add to casserole and mix in chopped carrot and celery.
Mix sauces, remaining marinade and water. Stir into pan, and scrape up the browning. Pour
into casserole. It should just cover ingredients. Add extra boiling water if necessary. Cover
firmly and simmer slowly in 275° oven for 3 to 3½ hours. (Lamb 2 to 2½ hours.) Skim off all
fat and sprinkle generously with chopped parsley before serving with vegetables.
Serves 7.*

91 EGMONT STEW

Similar in flavour to Scotch Broth.

Use scrag end neck, breast, flaps (or rib ends) left whole, and shank bones
of mutton.

Seasoning per pound:
1 teaspoon salt
1 clove garlic
freshly ground pepper
1 teaspoon honey
¼ teaspoon monosodium glutamate
¼ teaspoon grated nutmeg
1 or 2 bay leaves
parsley sprigs
1 small sprig rosemary
bacon rinds

1 large onion
1 large carrot
1 tablespoon soya sauce
1 tablespoon pearl barley
1 tablespoon split peas
milk and/or water
freshly ground pepper
1 tablespoon flour per cup of stock
squeeze lemon juice

Vegetables:
2 tablespoons butter
1 tomato peeled
1 small onion
1 small carrot
1 rib celery—some green top
2 tablespoons chopped parsley

2 tablespoons tomato pulp
½ teaspoon salt
1 teaspoon sugar
a good shake pepper
1 leek top—inner leaves

*Remove excess fat and leave joints uncut or in large pieces to fit neatly into a heavy-based
saucepan. Remove excess fat. Crush garlic with salt and pepper, mix with honey, glutamate
and nutmeg and rub into the meat. Stand up to 1 hour. Tie bay leaves, parsley and rosemary
into bouquet garni. Knot bacon rinds. Slice onion and carrot. Put all ingredients, except
flour and lemon juice, into a saucepan. Add sufficient milk and water to almost cover*

ingredients. Bring to boil. Reduce heat. Cover and simmer slowly 2½ hours. If the meat is separating from the rib bones before this, remove and put them aside. Skim off fat, or if possible, stand until next day and then lift off fat (in this case return ribs to cooling liquor). Otherwise cook 3 hours and skim off fat. Take meat from bones and cut into small pieces. Discard herb bouquet and bacon rinds. Almost cover meat with stock and slowly bring to boil. Mix flour and a little cold stock to a smooth paste and stir into the boiling stew. Simmer slowly while preparing vegetables.

Melt butter in saucepan until sizzling. Add vegetables, salt, sugar and pepper. Cover firmly. Reduce heat to a low simmer for 5 minutes.

Add to the simmering stew and after 20 to 30 minutes stir in lemon juice and serve with a purée of potatoes sprinkled with chopped parsley.

Serves 4 persons per lb meat.

Chapter 7

MINCE, MEAT LOAVES, PIES

92 BACHELOR'S MUTTON MINCE

$1\frac{1}{2}$ lbs mutton mince
1 teaspoon salt
pepper—a good shake
1 tablespoon flour
1 tablespoon onion soup powder
1 tablespoon sugar

1 teaspoon mustard
1 onion
3 tablespoons tomato sauce
$1\frac{1}{2}$ tablespoons soya sauce
boiling water

Thoroughly coat mince with mixture of salt, pepper, flour, soup powder, sugar and mustard. Use all of it and crumble into casserole or electric frying pan at 225°. Add chopped onion, sauces and water. Give mixture a good stir. Add other chopped vegetables if you wish.
Pre-heat oven to 225°. Cover and bake for $1\frac{1}{2}$ to $1\frac{3}{4}$ hours, or simmer slowly on top of stove.
Before serving, pour off fat and gather up residue with brown paper or a paper napkin.
Variation: Mix 1 or 2 tablespoons full cream milk powder to a paste with a little lemon juice or cider vinegar. Blend with a little mince gravy and then stir into mince. Pre-heat a minute or two before serving with vegetables.
Serves 5 to 6.

93 SAVOURY LOAF

$1\frac{1}{2}$ lb lean mutton
$\frac{1}{2}$ lb lean bacon (shoulder)
1 medium onion
1 cup breadcrumbs
2 tablespoons chopped parsley
1 teaspoon mustard powder
1 teaspoon dried basil
$1\frac{1}{2}$ teaspoons salt

$\frac{1}{4}$ teaspoon freshly ground pepper
$\frac{1}{4}$ teaspoon freshly grated nutmeg
1 tablespoon brown sugar
1 teaspoon grated lemon rind
2 teaspoons Worcester sauce
$\frac{1}{4}$ cup beer
$\frac{1}{4}$ cup water
1 tablespoon lemon juice

Mince together mutton, bacon and onion. Combine all dry ingredients, including lemon rind, and work them into meat mixture. Add Worcester sauce and beer diluted with water and lemon juice.
Pack mixture into a loaf pan and cover with tinfoil or buttered paper. Pre-heat oven to 325°.
Bake approximately $2\frac{1}{2}$ hours.
Remove loaf from oven. Place a warmed serving plate upside down on top and invert. Lift off pan. Serve hot or cold garnished with sliced or grated hard-boiled egg and chopped parsley.
To decorate when cold, see Chapter 10.
Serves 8.

94 MUTTON MOULD

Serve cold with salad

2 lb lean mutton
1 teaspoon salt
¼ teaspoon pepper
½ teaspoon sugar
4 oz lean shoulder bacon

1 cup savoury breadcrumbs (recipe 197)
¼ cup cold water
2 tablespoons cider vinegar
1 beaten egg
butter

Mince mutton, sprinkle with salt, pepper and sugar and mix.
Mince bacon and combine them. Stir in savoury breadcrumbs. Whisk cold water and vinegar
with egg. Stir into mince and press into a buttered bowl. Seal with tinfoil or buttered paper.
Place in saucepan in about 3 inches of boiling water. Cover and steam about 3 hours. Re-
plenish water when necessary. To remove bowl and decorate, see recipe 93.
Serves 8.

95 PICNIC LAMBURGERS

Delicious hot or cold. May be made the previous day

1 lb lean lamb or hogget from shank
   end of leg
2 cloves garlic
1¼ teaspoon celery salt
¼ teaspoon paprika
1 teaspoon coriander
1 teaspoon mustard
2 tablespoons of peach or apricot jam
2 bacon rashers
1 medium onion
1 tablespoon lemon juice

1 tablespoon tomato sauce
1 tablespoon Worcester sauce
3-4 medium sized potatoes, boiled
pepper
1 teaspoon nutmeg
1-2 tablespoons cream or top milk
2 tablespoons chopped parsley
flour
breadcrumbs
corn oil or lard

Coating : beat—
2 eggs
2 teaspoons corn oil
squeeze lemon juice

2 tablespoons water
salt
pepper

Slice meat and remove fat. Sprinkle well with garlic crushed with celery salt, paprika, corian-
der and mustard. Spread with jam. Put through the mincer three times. Add bacon rashers
and onion during the second grinding. Sprinkle with lemon juice, tomato and Worcester
sauces. Mash potatoes while hot with pepper, nutmeg, cream and chopped parsley. Cool a
little, then blend well with mince. Take rounded dessertspoons of mixture (or teaspoons if
small meatballs are required) and with floured hands gently shape as desired. Dip them in
egg coating and cover well with the crumbs. Finely chopped peanuts, almonds or grated
cheese may be added to crumbs.
Heat corn oil or lard to approximately 375°. Deepfry (see Glossary) until golden brown or
sauté in 1 inch hot corn oil. Turn to cook through and brown all round. Place on absorbent
paper to cool.
Makes 2 dozen substantial lamburgers or 4 dozen savoury meatballs.

96 MUTTON SAUSAGE MEAT

Suitable for breakfast or picnic lunches

1 lb raw lean mutton
2 bacon rashers (without rind)
1 teaspoon salt
½ teaspoon black pepper
dash of tabasco or red pepper sauce
¼ teaspoon marjoram
1 teaspoon mustard
1 teaspoon honey

1 teaspoon monosodium glutamate
3 tablespoons corn meal
2 tablespoons milk
flour
egg
breadcrumbs
cooking oil or bacon fat

Mince mutton and bacon twice. Add salt, pepper, sauce, marjoram, mustard, honey, glutamate, corn meal and milk, and pound well until consistency of sausage meat. With floured hands shape into sausages. Dip in beaten egg and coat with breadcrumbs.
Over moderate heat, sauté sausages in hot oil or bacon fat until golden brown and cooked through.
Alternatively smear loafpan with cooking oil. Press mixture therein. Paint generously with beaten egg, sprinkle with breadcrumbs and top with a few knobs of butter. Bake in oven at 300° for about 1½ hours.
Try one or more of the following additions: mushrooms, chopped; onion, minced; garlic chopped and crushed with salt; pineapple, grated; apple, grated; celery, grated; tomato pulp, strained.
Serves 4.

97 SHEEP'S HEAD PIE

Good hot or cold for picnics

1 sheep's head cooked (for preparation
   see Sheep's Head Soup, recipe 157)
2 bacon rashers
1 medium sized onion
1 rib celery
1 large tomato
1 teaspoon salt
pepper

1 cup tasty left-over gravy
¼ teaspoon mixed herbs
1 tablespoon tomato sauce
2 teaspoons Worcester sauce
pinch of sugar
1 packet flaky pastry or
   rough puff pastry (recipe 223)
2 hard-boiled eggs

Lift head from soup. When cool enough to handle take meat from the bones and discard the fatty tissue. Cut into cubes and mix with diced bacon, chopped onion, celery and peeled tomato. Sprinkle with 1 teaspoon salt and a good shake of pepper. Mix gravy with herbs, sauces and sugar, and add to meat.
Do not quite halve the pastry. Roll the larger piece and line a flan tin. Fill with mixture and top with sliced eggs. Cover with pastry, fold it over the lower crust, seal and flute.
Pre-heat oven to 450° and place pie above the centre for 7 minutes. Reduce heat to 325° and bake another ½ hour.
Variation: For a family luncheon dish, dice the eggs and fold into the mixture. Bake uncovered in oven at 350° for about 45 minutes. It may first be topped with pre-cooked potatoes whisked with a little milk and butter until smooth.
Serves 4 to 6.

98 ADELAIDE'S MUTTON PIE

2 lb lean mutton steaks
1 clove garlic
1½ teaspoons salt
½ teaspoon freshly ground pepper
generous pinch mace
generous pinch marjoram
2 teaspoons honey
1 tablespoon lemon juice or
  2 tablespoons cider vinegar
2 large onions
stock or water

2 tablespoons butter
1 rib celery shredded
1 large carrot sliced
2 tablespoons chopped parsley or mint
½ teaspoon sugar
½ teaspoon salt
1 cup green peas
1 packet mushroom soup powder
1 packet short or flaky pastry, or
  pastry (Chapter 20)

Cut steaks ½ inch thick. Rub with seasoning of garlic crushed with salt, the pepper, mace and marjoram. Cube and sprinkle with honey mixed with lemon juice or vinegar. If possible stand about an hour. Put one chopped onion with meat in casserole and barely cover with stock or water. Cover casserole. Pre-heat oven to 250°. Allow lamb 1 hour; hogget 1½ to 2 hours; mutton 2½ hours. Skim off any fat.

In a heavy-based saucepan heat butter until it is just starting to brown. Add sliced onion, celery, carrot and parsley seasoned with sugar and salt. Reduce heat to slow simmer, cover and after 5 minutes stir in thawed peas. Mix the soup powder (or thickening, see Glossary), with a little of the hot stock and stir into casserole. Work the sweated vegetables and mint through mixture. Place a pastry rest (the height of the casserole) in the centre. Cover and seal with pastry. Flute with thumb and forefinger and decorate as you wish. Bake at 450°. When pastry is cooked reduce heat to 300 for another 35 minutes.

Serves 8.

Note: *Small new potatoes may be added to casserole before covering with pastry.*

99 CORNISH PASTIES

Filling:
1 lb lean hogget
1½ teaspoons salt
pepper
1 clove crushed garlic
pinch of marjoram
pinch of nutmeg

pinch of mixed herbs
1 large potato
1 medium onion
4 tablespoons left-over gravy
short pastry (Chapter 20)

Cut meat into small pieces. Mix with seasoning, crushed garlic, herbs, diced potato and finely chopped onion. Mix with gravy and stand while preparing pastry. Cut pastry rounds with small saucer. Place filling in centre, fold pastry over, moisten edges and press with fork to seal firmly. Prick in three places. Bake at 425° for about 10 minutes. Reduce heat to 325° and bake another 50 to 60 minutes.

Makes 6 pasties.

Note: *For pasties with pre-cooked mutton, use filling for Superior Mutton Pie (recipe 110).*

Chapter 8

ORIENTAL COOKERY (WITHOUT CURRY)

All ingredients must be prepared in advance, as in most instances the cooking time is very short. Meat and vegetables, both cut diagonally to the same size, are usually cooked separately. The cooking oil must be very hot before slices or slivers of lamb, hogget or mutton are added and the meat should be only just cooked. The heat must be maintained and the meat kept in gentle motion by lifting and stirring with a fork until the colour changes. The vegetables, too, should retain some of their natural crispness. For this reason ingredients are added in rotation, according to their specific cooking periods. Vegetables are seldom served alone.

Immediately before serving, combine meat and vegetables and quickly heat through. Sprinkle generously with freshly ground pepper.

Accompaniments: Boiled or pan-fried rice, recipes 218 and 219; or boiled or pan-fried noodles, recipes 220 and 222.

Garnishes: Parsley, chopped or sprigs; watercress sprigs; lemon slices; stuffed olives sliced; hard-boiled eggs sliced, chopped or grated, etc.

Sauces: Soya or tabasco.

To prepare meat: Unless lean meat is advocated, remove excess fat only.

With a very sharp knife slice the meat across the grain into steaks of the required thickness. Pound slices if necessary to reduce thickness and tenderise meat. Thoroughly mix and rub into each pound of lamb or hogget steaks:

1 teaspoon honey   1 teaspoon crushed green ginger root
1 tablespoon lemon juice   1 clove garlic pulped
1 level teaspoon mustard powder (optional)

Arrange in a pile and stand 4 to 8 hours. One teaspoon ground horseradish may substitute for mustard, and $\frac{1}{4}$ teaspoon of either marjoram or oreganum may be added.
Treat mutton steak the same way. Use vinegar instead of lemon juice and stand 8 hours or longer.
Immediately before cooking, unless using a specific recipe, sprinkle each pound of meat with 1 level teaspoon salt and 1 teaspoon monosodium glutamate.

Stock: Use good hot mutton or vegetable stock or soup powder as stock base. If using cornflour or soup-powder with the stock or water, mix as thickening (Glossary) and allow it to simmer at least 10 minutes before serving. Season to taste if base is water.

100 JAPANESE HOGGET

1½ lb hogget steak
2 large onions
1 large carrot
1 young turnip
1 leek with some inner green top
2 ribs celery
¼ lb green beans
2 tomatoes
¼ lb mushrooms
4 tender cabbage leaves

Sauce:
2 tablespoons butter
1 packet pea and ham soup powder or
   1½ tablespoons cornflour

1 clove garlic
1½ teaspoons salt
pepper
2 rashers bacon
2 tablespoons soya bean oil
3 tablespoons soya sauce
½ teaspoon sugar
1 can bamboo shoots
chopped parsley or chives

1 cup each of milk and water, or 1 cup
   each of tomato juice and water, or
   2 cups stock
salt
pepper

To prepare sauce, melt butter in saucepan. Mix in soup powder or corn flour until smooth and slowly stir in 2 cups liquid. Stir continuously until mixture is smooth and boiling. Season to taste (soup powder, or seasoned stock, or liquor from salted bamboo shoots require less salt) and simmer sauce very slowly until required.

Prepare vegetables, cut meat into slices ¼ inch thick. Remove fat from steaks and pound with mallet or rolling pin. Season each side with garlic crushed with 1 teaspoon salt and some pepper. Cut this and bacon into thin strips about ¼ inch by 1½ inches, (use sharp kitchen scissors).

Heat oil until very hot. Lightly brown finely sliced onions and add prepared meat and bacon. Lift and stir with fork until colour changes. Stir in soya sauce. Remove mixture and keep hot. If necessary add more oil to pan and reheat. Add washed and thinly sliced vegetables with a little water clinging. After 2 minutes add shredded cabbage and sprinkle with ½ teaspoon sugar, salt and a good shake of pepper. Lift and stir about 3 minutes before adding the meat. A minute later add strained bamboo shoots. Reheat and serve immediately sprinkled with chopped parsley or chives.

Serve with boiled rice, recipe 218.

Serves 6.

101 MUTTON, HOGGET OR LAMB CHOW MEIN

2 lb thin lean mutton steaks from
   shank end leg
1 large onion
1 cup mushrooms
2 tomatoes peeled
1 cup celery
1 green pepper
1½ cups young heart cabbage
¼ cup canned pineapple diced
1½ tablespoons mushroom soup powder
   or 1 tablespoon cornflour

2 cups boiling water
2 tablespoons cooking oil
salt
3 tablespoons butter
½ teaspoon sugar
pepper
3 tablespoons soya sauce
1 can bean sprouts (optional)
noodles or rice

Prepare steaks, vegetables and pineapple. Prepare stock and keep hot. In a large pan or heavy-based saucepan heat oil until very hot. Add meat seasoned with salt, and finely chopped onion. Lift and stir gently until pieces change colour. Remove and keep hot.

Heat butter in pan until it starts to brown. Sauté finely sliced mushrooms 1 to 2 minutes. Remove and keep hot. Season sliced tomato, shredded celery, green pepper and cabbage with ½ teaspoon salt, sugar and some pepper, add to pan and stir lightly with a lifting motion for about 2 minutes.

Add mushrooms, pineapple and soya sauce. Cover and simmer 2 minutes. Add drained bean sprouts. After 3 minutes quickly fold the meat and onion into the vegetables and pour over the stock. Give a good stir and sprinkle generously with freshly ground pepper.

Heat through and serve with either boiled noodles, recipe 220, or rice, recipe 218.

To garnish, sprinkle with one or more of the following: chopped chives, parsley, grated hard-boiled egg or slivered almonds.

Serves 7 to 10.

102 SWEET SOUR MUTTON

½ lb lean mutton	1 teaspoon salt
1 small onion	1 teaspoon monosodium glutamate
½ lb young green cabbage	2 teaspoons sugar
1 clove garlic	2 tablespoons vinegar
1 red pepper	1 tablespoon soya sauce
3 tablespoons soya bean oil or saffola	

Prepare paper-thin slices of mutton and sprinkle with ½ teaspoon salt. Cut into ¼ inch strips. Finely slice onion and cabbage. Crush garlic. Discard pepper seeds and shred.

When oil in pan is hot, add onion, meat, garlic and pepper. Mix and agitate for ½ minute. Add cabbage, sprinkle with salt, glutamate, sugar, vinegar and soya sauce. Stir well, reduce heat, cover firmly and simmer 3-4 minutes.

Note: Westerners may prefer to substitute 1 teaspoon paprika or a pinch of chilli powder for the red pepper.

Serves 3.

103 SUKI YAKI

1½ lb lean hogget steak	1½ teaspoons salt
2 tablespoons cooking oil	¾ cup mushroom or pea and ham soup
1 large onion	powder stock
1 green pepper	¼ cup soya sauce
3-4 ribs celery	1½ tablespoons sugar
¼ lb or 1 can mushrooms	black pepper—freshly ground
1 cup or 1 can green beans	spring onions with green tops sliced
½ lb young cabbage	

Sliver steak (see Glossary) Heat oil in large frying pan or heavy-based saucepan. Finely slice vegetables. Add onion, green pepper, celery, mushrooms and beans to hot oil.

Sprinkle with ½ teaspoon salt. Stir and sauté until heated and golden. Stir in the stock (1 tablespoon soup powder whisked with hot water or use liquor from canned mushrooms and beans) and cabbage.

Sprinkle meat with salt. Arrange over vegetables. Reduce the heat a little. Cover firmly and steam 5 minutes. Add soya sauce and sprinkle with sugar. Lift and stir while simmering about 5 minutes. The vegetables must be just cooked and yet retain some of their crispness. Serve on a bed of boiled rice. Sprinkle with pepper and garnish with spring onions.

Serves 8.

104 CHOP SUEY

1 lb lean lamb or hogget steak
¼ lb mushrooms
2 large onions
3 cloves garlic
1 green pepper
1 tablespoon green ginger root
1-2 cups celery
1-2 cups young cabbage
3 tablespoons soya bean oil

1½ teaspoons salt
¼ teaspoon freshly ground pepper
2 tablespoons soya sauce
2 tablespoons pea and ham soup powder
2 cups boiling water
2 cups canned bean sprouts
boiled rice or boiled noodles
lemon slices
parsley or chives

Prepare meat as described in the opening of this chapter, in 1½ by ¼ inch strips. Prepare vegetables, heat oil with salt and pepper in large frying pan or heavy-based saucepan. Add sliced mushrooms, saute and stir for about 2 minutes. Lift out with slotted spoon. Add meat, stir and lightly brown all over (2 or 3 minutes). Add onions, garlic, green pepper, green ginger and celery all finely sliced. Gently lift and stir for 2 minutes. Return mushrooms, stir well 1 minute. Add shredded cabbage and soya sauce and heat through.
Whisk soup powder thickening into the water and pour it over mixture. Reduce heat to slow simmer for about 5 minutes. Add bean sprouts and thoroughly heat 2 or 3 minutes. Sprinkle with pepper before serving with plain boiled rice or noodles, recipes 218 and 220. Garnish with lemon slices, chopped chives or parsley.
Serves 5.
One cup finely sliced young green beans may replace bean sprouts. Add with onion, etc.

105 INDIAN MUTTON PILAU

2 lb mutton from leg, lean cutlets or steak
3 teaspoons salt
good shake freshly ground pepper
4 oz ghee (see Glossary)
6 cloves garlic
6 cardamoms or 1 teaspoon dried powder
1 inch green ginger root

1 green pepper
1½ cups rice
2 oz sultanas
3 cups stock
2 large onions
2 oz slivered almonds

Place meat with 2 teaspoons salt and pepper in saucepan with sufficient water to barely cover. Put lid on and simmer slowly until tender, 2 to 2½ hours. Pour off stock into bowl and stand in cold water to set fat. Lift off when cold. In a large pan heat 3 oz ghee until sizzling and sauté finely sliced garlic, cardamoms, crushed and chopped ginger and sliced green pepper for 5 minutes. Sprinkle with ½ teaspoon salt and a good pinch pepper. Add rice and sauté slowly, stirring continuously for 5 minutes. Add sultanas and hot stock, cover and simmer until rice is cooked—approximately 10 minutes. In another pan heat remaining ghee and brown cubed meat, add to rice and heat thoroughly.
If necessary add more ghee. When sizzling hot, season and lightly brown sliced onions. Put to one side of pan. Lightly colour slivered almonds and stir into meat and rice mixture. Served topped wtih brown onions.
Serves 8.

Chapter 9

CURRIES

Mutton is the ideal meat for the delightful fragrance and sweet-sour flavour of spicy curry dishes. Steaks from leg or shoulder are excellent but cheaper cuts which require longer cooking are equally good, i.e. scrag end neck, middle neck, breast and flaps.

Remove excess fat and cut meat into 1 to $1\frac{1}{4}$ inch cubes or to suit. Curry powder should always be well cooked and added at the beginning with salt and cayenne pepper or chilli powder. Sweetening is optional. Sugar or golden syrup to taste. The flavour is enriched if the dish is cooked 1 or 2 days before it is required, and stored in refrigerator. The fat is then easily lifted off. Slowly reheat and simmer about 30 minutes before serving.

Tender palates require a curry of mild flavour, so reduce the amount of curry powder. In this case the turmeric could be increased. The cayenne pepper or chilli powder should be reduced or omitted, and fiery red peppers avoided. Sophisticated palates, however, may prefer the amounts of these ingredients to be increased.

Curry may be stored in a deep freeze and thawed before slowly reheating. (A little more salt may be required before serving.)

Any of the following are suitable additions:

Spices: Use sparingly. Flavours should enhance rather than predominate. Cinnamon; ground ginger or the green ginger root bruised and finely chopped; preserved ginger chopped; ground cloves; coriander; chilli powder; cardamom; turmeric and allspice.

Sauces: Soya, tabasco, red pepper, chutney, sweet pickles, pickled walnuts.

Vegetables: Onions, carrots, string beans, leeks, celery, peeled tomatoes, green peppers.

Fruit: Apples, pineapple, bananas, sultanas, seedless raisins. With pineapple and banana pieces, do not add until 20 minutes before cooking time is finished.

Stock or water: Use good stock (Chapter 19) or soup powders. Generously coat meat with flour or cornflour before browning, as curry should not be thickened later. Excessive liquor should be reduced by rapid boiling.

Coconut milk: Grate half a fresh coconut and soak with its milk in half a pint of boiling water. When cold, mash well and strain through a fine sieve. Add this liquor to the curry just before serving, and re-heat. The residue in the sieve may be gently toasted and served as a garnish or side dish. (Use $\frac{1}{2}$ cup of grated coconut as a substitute for fresh coconut.)

Serve with long grained rice, boiled or pan fried (Chapter 19).

Garnishes or side dishes: Serve at least three of the following in small bowls: a spicy chutney (always); lemon slices; slivered or chopped almonds toasted; roasted peanuts; crystallised fruits; diced pineapple; banana slices; a mixture of raisins, chopped onion and apple fried in sizzling butter; crumbled crisp bacon; grated coconut raw or lightly toasted; a crisp green salad.

106 MUTTON CURRY

2½ lb mutton steaks or neck and breast
3 tablespoons vinegar
2½ teaspoons salt
1 teaspoon chilli powder
4 tablespoons flour
3 tablespoons cooking oil or fat
5 large onions
4 cloves garlic
2 tablespoons curry powder (or to taste)
3 ribs celery
1 large carrot
3 large tomatoes peeled or 1 cup purée
2 tart apples
1 green pepper (optional)

1½ inches green ginger root or
   1 teaspoon ground ginger
½ cup sultanas
dash of chilli powder or cayenne
1 teaspoon ground coriander
1 teaspoon cinnamon
1 teaspoon cardamom
boiling stock or water
½ teaspoon freshly ground pepper
2 tablespoons soya sauce
2 or 3 bananas sliced, or equivalent
   amount of pineapple pieces
1 tablespoon sugar (or to taste)

*Chop meat into pieces and remove any excess fat. Sprinkle with vinegar. Lift and turn 2
or 3 times, and stand until vinegar is absorbed (approximately 1 hour). Sprinkle meat with
salt, chilli powder (a pinch for tender palates) and flour (use all of it).*

*Heat oil or fat in large pan. Add chopped onion and crushed garlic. Sprinkle with curry
powder and ½ teaspoon extra salt. Stir and fry until mixture starts to brown. Blend in
chopped celery, carrot, tomato, apple and green pepper. Tip into a large, heavy-based
saucepan and keep hot.*

*Add meat to the pan, and when evenly browned mix in the chopped ginger root, sultanas
and spices. Put these in saucepan with vegetables. Add some stock to pan and scrape up
all the browning. Stir in soya sauce and sugar. Pour mixture into saucepan. Add sufficient
stock or boiling water almost to cover ingredients.*

*Bring to boil. Cover firmly and reduce heat to a slow simmer. Cook cubed steaks 2 to 2½
hours, neck and breast etc 3 to 3½ hours. When meat is tender stir in coconut milk and
bananas and/or pineapple pieces. When curry simmers again remove from heat.*

*If serving immediately, skim off fat and absorb residue with a paper napkin. Serve very hot
with boiled rice, recipe 218. Garnish with lemon slices and chopped parsley.*

*Side dishes: small bowls of toasted coconut, fruit chutney, roasted peanuts and a green
salad.*

Serves 10.

107 PRE-COOKED MUTTON CURRIES

*Follow either : (1) Recipes 60 and 64. Simmer ¾ to 1 hour. (2) Janet's Curry, recipe 108, with
these exceptions : Do not boil the joint in water. Put cubed cooked meat, sprinkled with
1 teaspoon of salt, with onions and brown in hot butter. As stock, boil 1 cup each of beer,
left-over gravy and water. Season to taste. Add more water if necessary. Simmer curry
slowly ¾ to 1 hour. Serve surrounded with boiled rice and garnish with chopped parsley
and lemon slices. Serve a good fruit or mango chutney as a side dish. (3) Curry sauce,
recipe 174. When preparing, omit flour and milk. Increase curry powder to 1 tablespoon. As
stock, mix 1 packet of pea and ham soup powder with a little water and make up to 3 cups
with hot water. In hot butter, brown cubed meat with 2 sliced onions sprinkled with ½ teaspoon of salt etc. Add hot sauce to cover. Simmer about ¾ hour and serve as above.*

108 JANET'S CURRY

2 lb hogget or mutton
2½ teaspoons salt
6 large onions
1½ tablespoons curry powder
1 teaspoon cinnamon
1 teaspoon cardamom
1 teaspoon black pepper
1 teaspoon turmeric

2 cloves garlic
2 tablespoons soya sauce
1 tablespoon chopped green ginger root,
  or 1 teaspoon ground ginger
1 cup tomato purée
3 ribs celery
1 large carrot
½ lb young green beans

Put uncut meat in saucepan with 1 teaspoon salt, 1 sliced onion and sufficient water to just cover, and simmer 1 hour (mutton 1½ hours).

In a heavy-based saucepan, put about 3 tablespoons of fat skimmed from liquor. When hot, brown the sliced onions mixed with the remaining salt and curry powder for about 10 minutes, stir frequently. Mix in cinnamon, cardamom, black pepper, turmeric, garlic well crushed, soya sauce, ginger and tomato purée. Reduce heat to simmer.

Take meat from stock. Remove excess fat and cut slices across the grain about ¾ inch thick and add to onions, etc. Pour fat from stock. Pass ice cubes over the surface to gather residue. Boil rapidly to reduce a little.

Pour in sufficient reduced stock to cover ingredients. Add chopped celery and carrot. Simmer hogget 1½ hours (mutton 2 hours). Add sliced beans 10 minutes before serving with boiled rice, recipe 218.

Serves 8.

109 ORIENTAL CURRY

1 lb lean mutton
1 teaspoon salt
1 tablespoon cornflour
2 red peppers or chillies
1 green pepper
2 cloves garlic
1 large onion
½ cup desiccated coconut
1 small can tomatoes
1 small can cubed pineapple

1½ tablespoons ghee or butter
3 teaspoons curry powder
½ teaspoon ground ginger
½ teaspoon grated nutmeg
1 teaspoon fenugreek powder
1 teaspoon turmeric
2 tablespoons vinegar
¼ teaspoon almond essence
2 cups shredded cabbage

Cube meat and sprinkle with salt and cornflour. Remove seeds from peppers or chillies and shred them. Chop green pepper. Crush garlic. Slice onions. Heat coconut with 1½ cups cold water, simmer slowly about 3 minutes, and strain coconut milk. Drain canned tomatoes and pineapple. Reserve juice.

Heat ghee or butter and brown meat with curry powder and onion. Add red pepper or chillies, garlic, ginger, nutmeg, fenugreek and turmeric. Stir well and add green pepper, strained juices, coconut milk, vinegar and almond essence. Cover and simmer slowly 2 hours. Skim off any fat. Add tomatoes, pineapple and cabbage. Check seasoning and simmer another ½ hour.

Serve surrounded with boiled rice, recipe 218. Garnish with finely shredded green pepper.

Serves 6.

Chapter 10

PRE-COOKED MUTTON DISHES

THE COLD JOINT

For a special occasion the joint should be cooked the previous day. Use a recipe from Chapters 2, 3 or 11. A joint (not a crusty joint) may be attractively decorated; into a small cup put 1 teaspoon of gelatine and 2 tablespoons of warm water. Stand in a little hot water. When decorations (below) are ready and gelatine is completely dissolved use a brush to paint it on the joint surface, a small area at a time. Start to design immediately. Decorations will set in the gelatine.

Some suitable fruits and vegetables: pineapple rings with cherry in centre, pineapple cubes which may be halved; orange slices peeled, with no white pith; mandarin segments peeled; eggs hard-boiled, sliced or in wedges; stuffed olives halved or slices; green or red pepper, in strings or rings; tomatoes firm, red or orange; cheese, in fine strips or grated; parsley or chives chopped.

Place on serving dish with sprigs of parsley or mint and lemon slices. Include a green salad with accompaniments, also french dressing, recipe 184, or mayonnaise, recipe 182. Serve these separately, or sprinkle prepared salad with french dressing, and gently lift and fold to mix.

110 SUPERIOR MUTTON PIE

2 lb cooked lean mutton, hogget or lamb	2 rashers bacon
2 or 3 sheep's kidneys	$\frac{1}{4}$ teaspoon mixed herbs
flour	left-over gravy
butter or bacon fat	2 eggs hard-boiled
2 large onions	parsley
1$\frac{1}{2}$ teaspoons salt	pastry, short or rough puff (Chapter 20)
a good pinch pepper	

Cube meat. Remove membranes from kidneys, dice and sprinkle with flour. Heat fat in heavy-based pan. Add chopped onion. When it changes colour add kidneys. Season lightly, stir, and remove when brown. Brown seasoned meat, return kidney and onion, add chopped bacon and mixed herbs. Stir in sufficient left-over gravy, seasoned to taste, to almost cover meat. Tip mixture into casserole and place a pie funnel or pastry rest in centre. Top with sliced egg and sprinkle with chopped parsley.

Cover with pastry and damp edges to seal. Flute and decorate as desired.

Pre-heat oven to 450°. Bake until pastry is golden, about 7 minutes. Reduce heat to 325° for 1 hour.

Serves 6-7.

111 CORNISH PASTIES WITH PRE-COOKED MUTTON

Prepare filling as in recipe 110 and see Cornish Pasties, recipe 99.

112 MOUSSAKA

1-1½ lb cooked lamb
1 small marrow
butter
2 large onions
1 large carrot
2 ribs celery
1 teaspoon salt
pepper—a generous shake

1 packet mushroom soup powder
pinch marjoram
1 cup milk
1 pint tomato juice
½ teaspoon basil
2 teaspoons sugar
grated cheese

Remove any fat from lamb and cut in cubes. Also cube the peeled seeded marrow. Butter a large casserole and place 1 sliced onion on the bottom. Combine meat with remaining chopped vegetables and sprinkle with 1 teaspoon salt and a generous shake of pepper. Place in casserole.
Mix soup powder and marjoram in bowl with a little milk and then stir in remainder. Add tomato juice, basil and sugar. Mix and pour over meat and vegetables. Cover firmly. Seal lid with tinfoil if necessary. Bake in oven at 300° for 2 hours. Remove lid. Top with grated cheese and place under grill to melt and brown lightly.
Serves 4-6.

113 MUTTON WITH MARJORAM SAUCE

1½-2 lb cooked mutton
3 cups mutton stock
4 tablespoons fat from stock
salt
pepper
1 medium onion
1 rib celery with leaves
1 clove garlic

2 tablespoons tomato pulp or 1 tomato
½ teaspoon sugar
3 tablespoons flour
½ to 1 teaspoon marjoram to taste
4 bacon rinds
1 or 2 tablespoons chopped parsley
lemon juice to taste
cooked potatoes

Heat fat in pan. Add seasoned chopped onion, celery and crushed garlic. Simmer gently and add tomato pulp with sugar.
Gradually blend in flour and marjoram. Slowly add mutton stock stirring continuously until sauce is smooth and boiling.
Add knotted bacon rinds, chopped parsley and lemon juice. In buttered casserole place alternate layers of sliced, seasoned mutton and sliced potatoes. Gently mix in sauce. Cover and bake in oven at 325° approximately 1 hour. Discard bacon rinds.
Note: *This dish may also be simmered slowly on top of stove or in a double boiler.*
Serves 6.

114 POTATO AND MUTTON FRITTERS

½ lb lean cooked mutton
1 onion
1 rasher bacon
1 clove garlic
1½ teaspoons salt
¼ teaspoon pepper
pinch nutmeg
pinch cayenne

4 medium raw potatoes
2 eggs
2 tablespoons flour
1 tablespoon cider, or 1 tablespoon milk
1 tablespoon chopped parsley
flour
bacon fat, butter or cooking oil

Mince or dice meat, onion, bacon, and garlic together. Season with salt, pepper, nutmeg and cayenne.
Grate potatoes into a strainer to drain off any liquor. Combine ingredients with mixture of eggs beaten with flour and cider. Add parsley. With floured hands shape into flat cakes.
Sauté 10 minutes each side in hot fat or oil until golden brown or deep fry (see Glossary). Serve with tomato sauce.
Serves 4.

115 LAMB OR MUTTON HASH WITH BEER

Follow recipe 117. Instead of gravy, cream or stock add ¼ cup boiling lager beer, 1 teaspoon mustard powder and 1 heaped teaspoon brown sugar.

116 QUICK LUNCHEON DISH

2 cups minced cooked mutton
1 cup rice
1 egg
3 tomatoes
1 teaspoon salt
pepper
½ teaspoon sugar
½ teaspoon dried basil
3 tablespoons butter

1 clove garlic
1 large onion
1 teaspoon curry powder
¼ teaspoon mixed herbs
2 tablespoons grated cheese
pinch dried dill
1 tablespoon soya sauce or to taste
stock
chopped parsley

Boil rice for 10 minutes, recipe 218. Hardboil egg. Mince meat. Peel and slice tomatoes and season with salt, pepper, sugar, and basil.
Heat butter in heavy-based saucepan or frypan. Lightly sauté crushed garlic and sliced onion a minute or two. Sprinkle in curry powder, mixed herbs and strained rice. Gently stir a few minutes, and when rice is changing colour add chopped egg, cheese and dill. Stir well and add tomato.
Add more butter to pan if necessary, and fold in seasoned meat. Stir frequently and cook another 3 or 4 minutes. Add soya sauce and 2 or 3 tablespoons boiling stock. Reduce heat to a low simmer, cover firmly and leave 20 minutes or longer. Add a little more boiling stock if necessary. Sprinkle with chopped parsley before serving.
Note: *Any chopped left-over vegetables may be added with the soya sauce and heated before adding the stock.*
Serves 6-8.

117 LAMB OR MUTTON HASH

Winter fare

1 lb cooked lean mutton	1 lb potatoes
1 large onion	left-over vegetables (optional)
1 clove garlic	3 tablespoons milk
½ teaspoon salt	2 tablespoons butter
¼ teaspoon pepper	1 teaspoon celery salt
1 rasher bacon	pinch pepper
1 tablespoon tomato sauce	pinch nutmeg
2 teaspoons soya sauce	butter or cooking oil

Slice mutton, quarter onion, and pulp garlic with salt. Sprinkle with seasoning. Cut rind from bacon. Put these ingredients through mincer, using coarse blade. Mix with tomato and soya sauces.

Peel and boil potatoes in salted water. Drain and add milk and butter, celery salt, pepper and nutmeg. Beat until light and fluffy. Combine with meat and vegetables. If mixture seems too dry add a little left-over gravy, cream or good stock.

In a pan heat some butter, cooking oil or fat until very hot. Add mixture and flatten. When under-surface is crisp and brown, turn with fish slice. Serve when thoroughly heated and nicely browned and crisp on both sides.

Serves 4.

118 CREAMED LAMB WITH CUCUMBER

2 lb lean cooked lamb	a good pinch dill
3 spring onions and green tops, or	mint
1 small onion	1 or 2 tablespoons butter or
1½ teaspoons salt	cooking oil
pepper	2 oz cider vinegar
1 egg	white foundation sauce, recipe 171
1 or more cucumbers	lemon juice
¼ teaspoon nutmeg	parsley
¼ teaspoon basil	bacon rashers (optional)

Combine diced lamb and finely sliced onions. Season and stand. Hard-boil egg. Peel cucumbers, halve lengthwise. Remove seeds and cut into slices 1 inch thick. Season with nutmeg, basil, dill and a little chopped mint.

Heat butter in heavy-based saucepan. Add cucumber. Sprinkle with a pinch of salt and the vinegar. Cover and simmer very gently about 10 minutes.

Remove cover and slightly increase heat to a rapid boil to reduce the liquid a little. The cucumber should then be tender but must not brown. Reduce heat, lightly stir in lamb, cover and slowly heat.

Prepare white foundation sauce, and when it boils add chopped egg and squeeze lemon juice. Gently combine with lamb and cucumber, and allow flavours to blend in a double boiler for approximately 20 minutes.

Serve garnished with parsley chopped and/or crisp grilled bacon rolls.

Serves 8.

119 POTATO ROLLS

Pastry:

1½ cups cold mashed potato
4 level tablespoons flour
1 teaspoon salt
½ teaspoon nutmeg

1 or 2 tablespoons chopped parsley
1 teaspoon celery seed
2 tablespoons milk
1½ tablespoons butter

Filling:

1 cup cooked lean mutton finely diced
1 clove garlic
1 teaspoon salt
a good pinch pepper
1 rasher bacon
1 small onion
2 tablespoons grated cheese
¼ teaspoon mixed herbs

2 eggs
1 talbespoon tomato sauce
½ tablespoon Worcester sauce
1 tablespoon left–over gravy
melted butter
breadcrumbs
1½ lb lard, or cooking oil

To make pastry, warm milk and butter and mix with remaining ingredients to a firm dough of rolling consistency. Add more milk if necessary.

To prepare filling, mash garlic with salt and pepper. Add to meat with finely chopped bacon and onion, grated cheese and mixed herbs. Beat 1 egg in separate bowl. Combine with sauces and gravy and fold into meat.

On a floured board (or between plastic) roll pastry thinly. Cut into oblongs and paint with melted butter. Put a spoonful of filling on each oblong. Roll and seal ends. Beat 1 egg with dash of Worcester sauce. Dip rolls in this, coat with breadcrumbs, and deep fry.(See Glossary).

Use a slotted spoon to lower rolls into hot fat. Fry two at a time until nutty-brown. Lift out, and place on rack in oven at 200° to keep hot.

Potato rolls may be sautéed in hot oil until evenly browned. Reduce heat a little and leave until filling is cooked.

Approximately 10 rolls. Serves 5.

120 GRECIAN LAMB SALAD

1¼ cups cooked diced lamb
tender cabbage leaves, or lettuce leaves
celery
green pepper
cucumber
2 tablespoons olive oil
1 medium onion

1 clove garlic
1 teaspoon salt
¼ cup cider vinegar
3 teaspoons sugar
1 teaspoon ground horse-radish or mustard
chopped parsley
freshly ground pepper

Shred 2 cups cabbage and celery and the seeded green pepper, and dice unpeeled cucumber. Fold lightly to combine. Tip into stainless steel or other unbreakable dish, and chill in refrigerator.

In hot oil cook finely chopped onion, garlic crushed with salt, and lamb until onion is transparent, but not brown. Add vinegar, sugar and horse-radish, and allow to come to boil. Pour lamb mixture over cold salad and fold lightly to combine the ingredients thoroughly. Serve sprinkled with chopped parsley and pepper.

Serves 6.

121 MUTTON COLLOPS AND TOMATO SAUCE

1 lb cooked lean mutton
2 tablespoons peanut oil
½ teaspoon salt

pepper
flour or savoury breadcrumbs, recipe 197

Marinade:
¼ cup tomato sauce
1 tablespoon soya sauce

2 teaspoons grated onion

Cut mutton in neat, rather thick slices (collops) and marinate 15 minutes in mixed marinade.
Heat oil in pan. Season meat with salt and pepper. Coat with flour or crumbs. Sauté collops in very hot oil until thoroughly heated, crisp and golden. Allow 3 to 5 minutes each side. Serves 4.

Also see: **MINTED LAMB MOULD** recipe 133
LAMB SANDWICH FILLING, recipe 159
PRE-COOKED MUTTON CURRIES, recipe 107.

Chapter 11

PICKLED SHEEP MEATS

122 SHEEPS TONGUES

Basic cooking: *Put pickled tongues in saucepan with 1 large onion, 1 large carrot, 2 or 3 ribs celery (all vegetables chopped), a few whole peppercorns, cloves, ½ teaspoon of mixed herbs and several bacon rinds. Just cover with water. Bring to boil. Reduce heat. Cover and simmer slowly 3 hours (lambs' tongues 1½ hours). When cooked the skin peels off easily.*

Remove tongues and as soon as they are cool enough to handle, peel and remove fatty tissue and any cartilage. For sheeps tongues in aspic, recipe 129, or sheep tongue mould, recipe 131, strain and reserve about ½ pint of the liquid.

Fresh sheeps tongues; same procedure but include 1½ teaspoons salt for six tongues.

123 SHEEPS TONGUES IN PARSLEY SAUCE SUPREME

Make parsley sauce supreme, recipe 179. Add cooked peeled tongues, and cook in double boiler for ½ hour. Garnish with lemon slices.
Variations:
SHEEPS TONGUES IN MUSTARD SAUCE, *recipe 175.*
SHEEPS TONGUES IN CAPER SAUCE, *recipe 172.*
SHEEPS TONGUES IN ASPIC, *recipe 129.*
SHEEPS TONGUE MOULD, *recipe 131.*
CANNED TONGUE MOULD, *recipe 132.*

To salt (pickle) mutton joints: *(If the order is placed in advance, a butcher will salt a mutton joint.) Either brine is suitable.*
Use an earthenware (stone crock), enamel (not chipped), glass or wooden vessel. Never use a metal container. Joints (removal of bone optional) should be at room temperature.

124 BRINE (I)

4 pints cold water	½ cup sugar
1 cup medium coarse salt (not iodised)	12 peppercorns
1 teaspoon baking soda	3 cloves garlic
1 teaspoon saltpetre	3 bay leaves

Stir dry ingredients into cold water until thoroughly dissolved. Add peppercorns, crushed garlic and bay leaves. Immerse a fresh joint of hogget or mature mutton, either whole or boned and rolled, in the pickle. To keep meat submerged, cover with a plate (not metal) and weight it. Cover with muslin and stand in a cool place.
After forty-eight hours remove meat and wash well under running water before cooking, see recipes 22 and 26.

125 BRINE (II)

2 gallons water
2 lb common salt (not iodised)
1 cup sugar

2 teaspoons baking soda
2 teaspoons saltpetre

Method I: Stir ingredients until thoroughly dissolved. Boil brine two or three minutes. When cold immerse mutton joints. Do not use a metal container. To keep them submerged, cover with china plate and weight it. Cover with muslin and stand in cool place. Soak joints not less than forty-eight hours. They may remain in the pickle up to twelve days in a cool place. Wash under cold running water and soak in cold water from 2-2½ hours (depending upon time submerged) before cooking, recipe 26.

Method II: Mix brine ingredients. Stir until dissolved. Submerge mutton joint. Bring to boil for 1 minute and cool. To keep joint submerged cover with a plate (not metal) and weight it. Cover with muslin. Can be kept in a cool place up to six weeks. Wash under cold running water and soak in ample cold water for 12 hours before cooking.

To poach salt or pickled mutton or mutton ham, see recipe 26.

126 MUTTON HAM

For a small sum any bacon factory will cure and smoke a leg of mature mutton. Refrigerate or deep freeze—otherwise use within 14 days.

To home cure: (process takes 14 days)

8-10 lb leg mutton at room temperature
1 lb medium coarse (dairy) salt—
   not iodised
5 oz brown sugar
2 teaspoons saltpetre
2 teaspoons pimento (allspice) crushed

2 teaspoons mustard powder
2 teaspoons baking soda
½ teaspoon ground peppercorns
4 tablespoons honey

Reserve 2 oz salt, and thoroughly mix all ingredients except honey.

First day: *Rub leg with 2 oz salt, pushing well down shank bone and into cavities. Hang over receptacle to catch drips.*

Second day: *Wipe off any moisture with dry cloth. Spread one tablespoon honey over joint and rub in. Then spread with a quarter of the salt mixture and thoroughly rub this in. Pay special attention to cavities. Lay joint on flat plate (not metal), or in a wooden tub.*

Repeat this procedure for four days. All the honey and salt mixture should be used. Lengthy rubbing is unnecessary. Each day the leg should lie on the alternate side.

Turn and baste daily for the next nine days.

On the fourteenth day soak ham (to remove excess saltiness) for 4 hours in cold water with 2 teaspoons baking soda added per gallon.

Remove and wash well in lukewarm water, 90°F. Drain, dry and hang for three days in full current of air to dry thoroughly. Pepper well and hang in a cheese cloth or mutton bag.

127 BAKED MUTTON HAM

1 mutton ham
flour
1 tablespoon honey

1 tablespoon cider vinegar
1 tablespoon mustard

Soak ham about 8 hours in cold water. Drain. Cover and seal completely with tinfoil or flour and water paste. (Mix flour to a rolling consistency with a little less than half the quantity of water.)
Pre-heat oven to 225°. If heat is from below, place as high as possible in oven. Bake approximately 60 minutes per pound.
When cooked remove covering and rest ham on rack in the baking pan. With a sharp knife cut a diamond criss-cross pattern through the upper skin and into the fatty tissue.
Mix honey, cider vinegar and mustard. Spread glaze over ham and place under grill— not too close to heat—until nut-brown and crisp.

128 GENTLE HERB PICKLE FOR MUTTON

For each pound of meat allow:
small sprig rosemary
small sprig thyme
a few parsley leaves and stems
$\frac{1}{2}$ clove garlic
1 drop or to taste oil of pine
  (from chemist)

1 drop or to taste oil of almond
  (from chemist)
1 teaspoon common salt
2 teaspoons honey
1 teaspoon vinegar
$\frac{1}{2}$ cup light beer
1 packet onion soup powder
pepper, freshly ground
4 tablespoons soured cream

For a 4-pound shoulder mutton, for example, increase the above ingredients four-fold.
Pound herbs and oils to a pulp in bowl with wooden spoon or pestle. Mix in the salt until pickle is green. Stir in honey and vinegar.
Lay the joint on a flat plate and coat evenly with pickle. Thoroughly rub into meat and let it stand for two days. Turn and baste well once or twice a day.
Pre-heat oven to 300°. In a roasting pan (with tight lid) sprinkle 1 packet onion soup powder. Place joint on this and pour over any remaining honey mixture. Cover firmly and bake in oven until tender. Allow 35-45 minutes per pound.
Remove joint. Sprinkle generously with freshly ground pepper and keep warm. Skim fat from liquor. Stir in beer. Boil 2 or 3 minutes. Add cream and pepper. Re-heat and serve gravy separately.
Alternative: Into the liquor stir a little flour and water paste until smooth. Add some stock if necessary, and simmer slowly about 10 minutes.

Chapter 12

MUTTON AND LAMB IN ASPIC

General method:
Slice thinly, cube, dice, mince or sliver pre-cooked:

lean mutton or lamb	mutton ham
sheeps tongues	liverwurst
meat loaf	picnic lamburgers or sausage meat

Combine or arrange in alternate layers with some of the following (pre-cooked if necessary), sliced or diced, etc: eggs, hardboiled; asparagus; green peas; green beans; red beet (raw or cooked); onion; cucumbers; tomatoes; nuts; pineapple (canned); chopped parsley; chopped mint; chopped chives; cauliflower florets; gherkins; canned peaches or other stone fruit; carrots (raw or cooked); celery; radishes; green peppers; pickles; olives; capers; shallots or spring onions with some green top.

Note: Raw pineapple and chinese gooseberries cannot be used in aspic as gelatine will not set.

When using gelatine the measurements must be exact: 10 tablespoons liquid = 5 oz = ¼ pint.

Three level teaspoons gelatine or 1 envelope will be sufficient to firmly set ¾ pint liquid. Dissolve gelatine in a little cold water and thoroughly stir in the hot liquid.

To decorate mould: Dissolve 1 teaspoon gelatine in 2 tablespoons of hot water and stand cup in hot water. Put a thin layer in bottom of mould and sprinkle lightly with chopped parsley. Arrange a design with slices of egg and any of the above. Cover thinly with gelatine. Paint the sides of the mould and continue the design. When firm, carefully arrange solids and pour in liquid. Chill until set.

To unmould: Remove from refrigerator an hour before required. Run the point of a warm knife around edge of mould. Then stand mould in warm (blood heat) water a few seconds. Quickly dry mould. Place serving dish on top, invert and shake gently.

Servings depend on size of mould.

129 SHEEPS TONGUES IN ASPIC

12 tongues, cooked and peeled, recipe 122	2 eggs
gelatine	a few stuffed olives
½ pint strained stock from tongue liquor	parsley

Hardboil eggs. Soak 1 teaspoon gelatine in tablespoon cold water until dissolved. Stir in 2 tablespoons hot stock and keep warm. Chop parsley, slice eggs and olives. Decorate mould in an attractive design.

Dissolve 1½ teaspoons gelatine in a little stock, add the rest and stir well. Gently arrange tongues in mould. Give stock another stir, and pour into mould. Place small flat plate on top and weight it. Chill, and when aspic is set, remove weight. Unmould and serve with crisp green salad.

Serves 10-12.

130 GRETCHEN'S MUTTON BRAWN

4 mutton shanks
1 pig's trotter
3 sheeps tongues } from brine
  (or 1 can sheep's tongues)
1 large onion
a few peppercorns
a few cloves

a few allspice
1-2 ribs celery
a few bacon rinds
1 hard-boiled egg
parsley

Put meat, onion, spices, celery, and knotted bacon rinds into saucepan and cover with cold water. Bring to boil and simmer slowly until very tender—about 3½ hours. Lift meat from liquor and remove bones. Peel tongues while hot. Remove any fatty tissue and cartilage. Cut into round pieces. Strain stock and boil rapidly until reduced to half quantity. Add meat and simmer slowly half an hour. If using canned tongues, include the melted aspic. Pour into mould to set.
To decorate mould and to unmould: *See preceding directions.*
Use egg and parsley for decoration. Serve surrounded with salad.
Serves 7.

131 SHEEPS TONGUE MOULD

3 sheeps tongues, cooked and peeled,
  recipe 122
2 eggs
3 teaspoons gelatine
1 tablespoon chopped parsley
pinch mustard powder
pinch horse-radish

¼ teaspoon lemon rind
1 teaspoon lemon juice or cider vinegar
½ pint tongue stock (strained)
1 tablespoon onion
pepper

Hard-boil eggs and slice. Dissolve 3 teaspoons powdered gelatine in 5 tablespoons hot water. Stir and put 2 teaspoons liquid gelatine in base of mould. Sprinkle with a little chopped parsley, and arrange half the egg slices on this. Mix mustard, horse-radish, lemon rind and juice, and add to gelatine. Stir in stock, finely chopped onion, parsley and generous shake of freshly ground pepper. Peel tongues while hot, then cool, slice in rounds, and arrange in mould with remaining egg slices. Gently pour in liquor. Chill until firm. Unmould. Before serving surround with salad greens.
Serves 3.

132 CANNED TONGUE MOULD

Melt aspic from can. Measure hot water or stock to increase liquor to ½ pint. Season to taste. Stir in sufficient dissolved gelatine (see preceding directions). Follow recipe 131.
One tongue per serving.

133 MINTED LAMB MOULD

1 lb lean lamb (cooked)
2 eggs
3 teaspoons gelatine
2 or 3 spring onions with green tops

1 tablespoon lemon juice
1½ teaspoons sugar
1 teaspoon salt
¼ cup chopped mint

Hard-boil eggs and cool. In a breakfast cup dissolve 3 teaspoons gelatine in 2 tablespoons cold water. Fill cup with boiling water or clear tasty stock, and stir well. Cube or dice lamb, and arrange alternate layers of sliced egg, onion and meat in mould. Add lemon juice, sugar, salt and mint to gelatine liquor. Pour into mould and chill until firm. Unmould and surround with crisp lettuce leaves, wedges of tomato, cucumber slices and finely chopped chives.
Serves 4.

Chapter 13

LIVER, KIDNEYS, HEARTS, BRAINS, SWEETBREADS

134 LAMBS' FRY SAUTE

1 lb lambs' fry
1 teaspoon salt
pepper
pinch of majoram
flour

cooking oil, butter or bacon fat
4 rashers bacon
½ cup red wine (optional)
cream

Remove membrane and bloodvessels from fry and cut slices about ⅓ inch thick. Sprinkle with salt, a good shake pepper, majoram and flour.

Heat oil in pan. Brown slices 3-4 minutes each side (they will harden if overcooked). To avoid this, after turning, make a gash in the centre of one slice to half its depth. As soon as the colour changes, remove slices to serving dish. Cover, keep warm, and serve as soon as possible.

On a grilling rack overlap the bacon rashers to cover the lean meat. To prevent curling nick the fatty edges in several places. Place under pre-heated grill until crisp. Watch carefully. Arrange around fry.

Thoroughly scrape up the pan browning with ½ cup of red wine or water. Boil rapidly a few seconds. Reduce heat, check seasoning and stir in 1-2 tablespoons cream. Reheat and serve.

Alternative: *In the pan browning, blend 1 tablespoon of flour, ½ teaspoon of salt, a pinch of sugar and a shake of pepper. Slowly stir in 1 cup of cold water. Boil. Reduce heat and simmer 10 minutes.*

Note: *If this dish must wait, add fry to gravy. Cover with firm lid and keep hot at low heat.*
    Serves 4.

135 SHEEPS FRY IN MARINADE

1½ lb liver (fry)
1½ cups milk
2 ozs red wine
1½ teaspoons salt
pepper

flour
2 tablespoons butter
2 onions
¼ lb mushrooms (optional)
6 bacon rashers

Boil milk and cool it. Remove membrane and bloodvessels from liver. Cut slices about ½ inch thick and place in bowl. Cover with milk and wine, and marinate up to 8 hours. Drain liver and reserve marinade. Season and flour generously.

Heat butter in pan and gently sauté sliced onions a minute or two. Add sliced mushrooms, and when tender sprinkle with a pinch of salt and pepper. Do not brown. Remove and keep hot.

Increase heat, and when butter is starting to brown, sauté liver 3-4 minutes each side. Remove and keep warm with onions and mushrooms. Pour marinade into the pan. Scrape up all browning. Stir and boil rapidly ½ minute. Reduce heat. Season to taste.

Return fry to pan. Top with onions and mushrooms, cover firmly and simmer very slowly 20 to 30 minutes. Serve with grilled bacon rashers.
    Serves 6.

136 SHEEPS LIVER AND ONIONS ITALIAN STYLE

1 lb liver
¼ cup claret or dry red wine
4 medium onions
peanut oil

1 teaspoon salt
¼ teaspoon pepper
flour
1 tablespoon cream

Cut liver into 8 thin slices. Add wine and marinate at least 1 hour. Turn occasionally.
Sauté sliced seasoned onions in hot oil until lightly browned. Remove and keep hot.
Drain liver slices. Season with salt and pepper. Roll in flour and sauté each side 4-5 minutes
in the hot oil. Remove and keep hot. Add wine to the pan and simmer a few seconds to
dissipate alcohol. Stir well to scrape up the pan browning. Reduce heat and stir in 1 table-
spoon cream. Reheat gravy. Serve in separate dish.
   Serves 4.

137 GREENMEADOW LAMBS' FRY

1 lamb's fry
1 teaspoon salt
¼ teaspoon black pepper
¼ teaspoon marjoram
flour
bacon fat

1 large onion
bacon rashers
tomatoes
½ teaspoon sugar
½ teaspoon basil

Stuffing:
1 cup breadcrumbs
1 inner rib celery shredded
1 small onion chopped
1 tablespoon grated cheese
¾ teaspoon salt

pepper
pinch sage
pinch thyme
¼ cup stewed apple, sweetened to taste
1 small egg

Stuffing: *Mix dry ingredients, combine with drained apple and 1½ tablespoons beaten egg.*
Slit fry about 3 inches along the thick side and cut a deep pocket. Lightly fill with stuffing
and close slit securely with safety pins. Sprinkle all over with mixture of salt, pepper,
marjoram and flour.
Coat baking dish with bacon fat or equivalent and cover the base with sliced onion. Place
fry on this. Cover with rindless bacon rashers, 1 per serving. Top with a thick layer of sliced
tomatoes. Sprinkle with a pinch of salt and pepper, the sugar and basil. Cover and bake
in oven at 325° for approximately 1½ to 2 hours, depending upon the size of the fry. Serve
with sautéed mushrooms.
   Serves 4 per lb.

138 LIVER PATTIES
Delicious hot or cold for picnics

1 lamb's fry
½ lb lean bacon or meat from ham hock
1 medium onion
2 tablespoons parsley
1 teaspoon salt
¼ teaspoon pepper

1 teaspoon mustard
¼ teaspoon marjoram
1 large apple
½ cup soft breadcrumbs
1 small egg
flour
olive oil

Mince liver, bacon and onion twice. Add parsley, salt, pepper, mustard and marjoram. Peel apple and grate over the mixture. Add breadcrumbs and beaten egg to bind. Combine well.

With floured hands shape into balls and deep fry in about 4 inches very hot oil, or sauté in about $\frac{1}{4}$ inch hot oil until crisp, nicely brown and cooked through.

Serves 6 to 7.

Also see : **LIVER SANDWICH PASTE,** recipe 162.
    LIVER AND MUSHROOM FILLING, recipe 164.

139 LIVERWURST, HOMEMADE

Excellent hot or cold for parties or picnics

1 lb liver	1 teaspoon mustard
$\frac{1}{4}$ lb shoulder bacon without rinds	$\frac{1}{4}$ teaspoon marjoram
1 clove garlic	dash of tabasco sauce
$1\frac{1}{4}$ teaspoons salt	3 tablespoon soured cream
good pinch black pepper	4 tablespoons cornmeal
2 teaspoons brown sugar	flour

Remove membrane and bloodvessels from liver. Put the liver, bacon and garlic through the mincer three times. Add salt, pepper, sugar, herbs and sauce to soured cream. Pour over the mince and pound to fine pulp. Mix in the cornmeal thoroughly.

Using floured board and floured hands, gently form liverwurst roll about 2 inches in diameter. Either encase the whole in a flour and water paste (rolled $\frac{1}{8}$ inch thick) or seal in tinfoil. Bake in pan in oven at 350° for 1 hour.

Open. Serve hot topped with grated hard-boiled egg and chopped parsley. Serve cold as a loaf decorated with sliced egg, parsley and surrounded by salad.

Serves 6.

140 SHEEPS KIDNEYS SAUTE

kidneys (2 per serving)	flour
2 teaspoons lemon juice or vinegar	butter
$\frac{1}{4}$ teaspoon salt	2-3 tablespoons madeira or sherry
good shake pepper	bacon rashers
a pinch marjoram	

Remove membrane and halve kidneys. Sprinkle with lemon juice or vinegar. Season and flour well. (Amounts listed are sufficient for 2 kidneys.) Sauté each side about 2 to 3 minutes in hot butter until just cooked. Add wine or stock to pan and allow to bubble a second or two. Reduce heat. Put kidneys on serving dish and keep warm.

Scrape up the pan browning and stir in 2 tablespoons of cream. Season to taste and allow to simmer half a minute. Serve with kidneys and crisp grilled bacon rashers.

Note: Sauté lambs kidneys $1\frac{1}{2}$ to 2 minutes each side, and thinly sliced kidneys until each side changes colour.

141 SHEEPS KIDNEY SNACK OR FILLING

6 kidneys
1 small onion
2 oz mushrooms
1 teaspoon salt
a good pinch pepper
a good pinch marjoram
flour

2 tablespoon butter
½ rib celery
1 tomato, or 2 tablespoons purée
½ teaspoon sugar
3 tablespoons madeira or sherry
4 tablespoons cream
1 tablespoon chopped parsley

Peel and halve kidneys, remove fat and dice them. Mix with chopped onion and mushrooms. Sprinkle with seasoning and flour well. Heat butter until it starts to brown. Add mixture. Stir and brown a little. Remove and keep warm. Reduce heat and add shredded celery, chopped tomato and sugar. Cover and simmer slowly about 10 minutes. Return kidney, etc. When heated through stir in wine and bring to boiling point. Reduce heat, stir in cream and parsley. Simmer very gently 10 to 20 minutes to enrich flavour. Serve on croutes (see Glossary).
Serves 4.

142 LUNCHEON KIDNEYS WITH MUSHROOMS

6 sheeps or lambs' kidneys
1 teaspoon salt
pepper
flour
2 tablespoons butter

1 onion
2-4 oz mushrooms
1 tablespoon mushroom soup powder
1 cup hot water
4 bacon rashers

Soak kidneys in warm salty water ½ hour. Dry and peel them, halve and remove fat. Cut each half into 4 slices and sprinkle lightly with salt, a generous shake of pepper and flour. In sizzling butter sauté the sliced onion until it starts to brown, and stir in the peeled and sliced mushrooms. Season lightly, and after a minute move to one side of pan. Sauté kidney slices each side until they change colour. Reduce heat. Mix soup powder with cold water, stir into hot water and pour into pan. Cover and simmer slowly about ten minutes. Serve with grilled bacon rashers.
Serves 4.

SHEEPS HEARTS

Basic Preparation: Remove scraggy tops. Trim cavities. Sprinkle with salt and stand about 30 minutes. Wash under cold running water and dry.

143 SAUTE HEARTS

2 sheeps hearts	1 tablespoon bacon fat or cooking oil
salt	1 cup stock or water
pepper	3 bacon rashers
flour	

Follow basic procedure page 87. Cut hearts in rounds about ¼ inch thick. Sprinkle with 1 teaspoon salt, some pepper and flour. Put oil and 1 dessertspoon flour in pan and cook over moderate heat until lightly brown. Add heart slices and sauté each side about 5 minutes. Lift out and keep warm.

Blend 1 tablespoon flour with pan drippings and slowly stir in stock until it boils. Reduce heat and check seasoning. Return meat to pan, and simmer slowly 10 minutes or longer. Serve with grilled bacon rashers.

Serves 3.

144 ROAST HEARTS

3 sheeps hearts	1 tablespoon butter
Red wine stuffing, recipe 198	flour
1 clove garlic	bacon fat
1½ teaspoons salt	tinfoil
pepper	3 bacon rashers

Prepare hearts for cooking—see preceding directions on page 87. Make half the quantity of stuffing and lightly fill cavities. Seal with plugs of tinfoil or safety pins or sew up with thread. Rub with garlic crushed with salt and pepper. Spread upper surfaces with softened butter, coat all over with flour.

Put fat with 1 tablespoon flour in roasting pan, add hearts and cover with tinfoil. Put pan high in oven pre-heated to 300°. Bake lambs' hearts 1½ hours, sheeps' hearts 2 hours or longer. They must be well cooked.

Remove tinfoil. Place hearts on a fireproof plate, cover with pieces of bacon overlapped, and place under grill until crisp.

Prepare gravy, recipe 170.

Serves 4 (lambs' hearts 3).

SHEEPS BRAINS

Basic preparation: Into a cup of lukewarm water, stir 2 teaspoons of salt until dissolved and soak brains for 30 minutes. Wash under cold running water.

Put brains in a small saucepan, just cover with cold water and a squeeze of lemon juice or a few drops of vinegar. Bring to boil. Simmer slowly 5 minutes, lift out and peel off any loose membrane.

145 SAUTEED SHEEPS BRAINS

2 sets brains
¾ teaspoon salt
pepper
flour
1 egg

breadcrumbs
butter
3 bacon rashers
lemon slices

Prepare brains as on previous page. Dry and section, then sprinkle with salt and pepper, and coat with flour. Dip in beaten egg and roll in breadcrumbs.
Heat butter until it starts to brown. Sauté brains until the coating is evenly browned and crisp.
Serve with grilled bacon rashers. Garnish with lemon slices and tiny sprigs of parsley.
Serves 3.

146 CREAMED SHEEPS BRAINS

Make Parsley Sauce Supreme, recipe 179.
Follow basic preparation, then break brains into bite-size pieces, and add one or two pieces at a time to sauce to prevent it going off the boil (or first transfer sauce to double boiler). Reduce heat to a slow simmer for about 15 minutes until brains are thoroughly cooked.
Garnish with lemon slices.

147 BRAIN FRITTERS

3 sets brains
2 rashers lean bacon
1 egg hard-boiled
½ clove garlic
½ teaspoon salt
pepper

1 tablespoon chopped parsley
2 teaspoons grated onion
squeeze lemon juice
parsley
lemon slices
cooking oil or bacon fat

Batter:
4 tablespoons flour
½ teaspoon salt
¼ teaspoon pepper

1 egg
½ teacup milk

To prepare brains follow the basic procedure, then pulverise with minced bacon rashers, egg, garlic (chopped and crushed with salt), pepper, parsley, onion and lemon juice; (or finely chop brains and egg, and combine with other ingredients).
To prepare batter: Sift dry ingredients, make a well in centre. Add egg and milk. Beat until thick and creamy.
In a heavy-based pan heat oil or bacon fat or lard until very hot. Fold brain mixture into the batter and drop heaped teaspoonfuls into hot oil. Turn when under-surface is crisp and golden. Give fritters sufficient time to cook through, approximately 5 minutes each side. Or, with well-floured hands roll the brain mixture into small balls. Flatten a little and dip in batter. Spoon into hot oil and sauté as above or deep fry.
Keep hot on absorbent paper and serve as soon as possible. Garnish with sprigs of parsley and lemon slices.
Serves 6.

148 BRAIN AND MUSHROOM SAVOURY

3 sets brains	2 teaspoons grated onion
2 rashers lean bacon	squeeze of lemon juice
1 egg	1 tablespoon butter
$\frac{1}{2}$ clove garlic	1 packet mushroom soup powder
$\frac{1}{2}$ teaspoon salt	pinch of marjoram
pepper	$\frac{1}{2}$ cup milk
parsley	cream

Prepare brains as directed. Mince bacon and combine with finely chopped brains and hard-boiled egg, garlic crushed with salt, the pepper, parsley, onion and lemon juice. In a small saucepan melt the butter until it starts to brown. Blend in the soup powder, marjoram and brain mixture. Slowly stir in the milk. Bring to boil, then reduce heat and simmer slowly about 10 minutes. Stir in a little cream and simmer another minute. Serve hot on croutes. Top with chopped parsley.

For a quick luncheon or supper snack, use as a filling for sautéed sandwiches, see recipe 168. Serves 4.

LAMBS' OR SHEEPS SWEETBREADS

Basic procedure : Soak sweetbreads in lukewarm water with a little vinegar and salt for half an hour or longer. Wash, put sweetbreads in saucepan with:

juice of $\frac{1}{2}$ lemon	pinch of mace or nutmeg
a little grated lemon rind	1 teaspoon salt
1 small onion grated	pepper—a generous shake

Cover with water. Bring to boil and simmer slowly for 15 minutes. (Spring lamb 5 minutes). Reserve stock. Immerse sweetbreads in cold water for about 10 minutes. Peel off membranes and remove fat. Lift fat from cool stock.

Spring lamb sweetbreads may be floured and sautéed in hot butter until lightly browned or see recipe 145.

149 SCALLOPED LAMBS' SWEETBREADS

For a special occasion

6 sweetbreads	baked breadcrumbs
reserved stock	1 egg white
1 teaspoon salt	butter and cooking oil
$\frac{1}{4}$ teaspoon pepper	3 bacon rashers
flour	parsley

Sauce :

3 tablespoons butter	1 tablespoon sherry
3 tablespoons flour	squeeze of lemon juice
1 cup cooking liquor	1-2 tablespoons cream
1 egg yolk	

Follow basic preparation procedure. Boil the skimmed stock, add sweetbreads, cover and slowly simmer hogget 1$\frac{1}{2}$ hours; sheep 2 hours. Take sweetbreads from stock, dry them and sprinkle with seasoning and flour.

To prepare sauce, melt the butter. Blend in the flour until smooth and slowly add cooking liquor. Stir briskly until thickened and simmer slowly 10 minutes. Whisk in the egg yolk. Add sherry and lemon juice. Check seasoning and stir in 1 to 2 tablespoons of cream.

Put a generous layer of breadcrumbs on a flat plate. Heavily coat one side of sweetbreads with sauce and place on breadcrumbs. Mask with sauce, then breadcrumbs. Reserve the remaining sauce. Stand at least one hour until cold. (Sweetbreads may be prepared to this stage the day before required, in which case keep egg-white airtight.) Brush all over with egg-white and again sprinkle with breadcrumbs.

Heat equal quantities of hot butter and cooking oil. Sauté each side of sweetbreads until golden brown, crisp and thoroughly heated.

Grill bacon rashers. Thin the sauce with a little skimmed stock and cream. Heat and serve separately.

Serve sweetbreads with halved tomatoes and mushrooms, grilled or sautéed, potato puree and green peas. Garnish with chopped parsley.

Serves 3.

Party Snacks: Follow above recipe with this addition: after simmering sweetbreads 1½ to 2 hours lift from cooking stock and place between plates. Put a weight on top as a press. When cold, dry and with a sharp knife halve, cube or slice sweetbreads before seasoning, etc.

150 SWEETBREAD PÂTÉ

1 lb sheep's sweetbreads
1 teaspoon salt
¼ teaspoon pepper
sauce

2 tablespoons parsley
2 eggs hard-boiled
rough puff pastry

Follow recipe 149 with the following exceptions: after the basic procedure simmer sweetbreads in boiling stock ½ hour only. Drain (reserve stock), cool a little and break into small pieces. Sprinkle with salt and pepper.

The sauce requires only 3 minutes simmering before whisking in the egg yolk. Fold in the parsley and warm sweetbreads. Line a shallow casserole or flan tin with pastry rolled ⅛ inch (reserve sufficient for top). Paint with a little egg-white and allow to dry. Add filling, cover with sliced eggs. Top with pastry and prick it with a fork in several places. Seal and decorate as desired. Bake at 450° for 7 to 10 minutes. Reduce heat to 300° for 1 hour.

Serves 6.

151 SWEETBREAD VOL-AU-VENT

sweetbread filling
1¼ lb rough puff pastry

2 tablespoons chopped parsley

Follow recipe 149 but simmer sweetbreads in skimmed stock for ½ hour only. Drain (reserve stock), season and keep sweetbreads warm. The sauce requires only 3 minutes simmering before whisking in the egg yolk, etc. Break sweetbreads into small pieces, add to the sauce and simmer in double boiler 1¼ hours. Add parsley.

Roll pastry ⅛ inch thick, 16 x 8 inches. Lift to allow air to pass beneath it. Cut 2 rounds (use a plate or lid 8 inches in diameter as guide). Place guide about 6½ inches in diameter in the centre of one circle, and cut round as top for vol-au-vent. Moisten edge of large circle, place ring of pastry evenly on this and press to seal. Place this and smaller circle on cold oven tray and stand in a cool spot 20 minutes. Pre-heat oven to 450° and bake 15-20 minutes. To serve: Pre-heat oven to 300°. Put vol-au-vent on heatproof plate and top on oven slide. Pastry and filling, with parsley added, are served piping hot. Be sure to fill immediately before serving. Use a fish-slice to manipulate the top.

Serves 6.

152 SAUTEED LAMBS' SWEETBREADS

8 sweetbreads
salt
pepper
flour
1 egg
1 tablespoon sherry

1 tablespoon stock
breadcrumbs
1 tablespoon cooking oil
1 tablespoon butter
4 bacon rashers

To prepare sweetbreads follow the basic procedure, then return them to the stock and simmer slowly for 1½ to 2 hours. Lift out, cool and dry.

Sprinkle sweetbreads with salt, pepper and flour. Dip in mixture of egg, beaten with sherry and stock. Coat with breadcrumbs. Repeat this step (optional). Sauté each side in hot oil and butter until nicely browned, crisp and thoroughly heated. Serve sweetbreads with grilled bacon and garnish with lemon slices and chopped peppers.

Serves 4.

153 CREAMED SWEETBREADS

Also suitable as a filling for savouries, sautéed sandwiches or on croutes

1 lb sweetbreads
2¼ tablespoons butter
2 teaspoons grated onion
1 tablespoon (heaped) chopped parsley
salt
pepper
2¼ tablespoons flour

pinch nutmeg
½ teaspoon sugar
½ cup top milk
½ cup stock
1 tablespoon sherry
squeeze of lemon juice

To prepare sweetbreads follow basic procedure (reserve ½ cup stock) then break into small pieces. Melt butter in the top of a double boiler. Add onion, parsley, a pinch of salt and pepper. Cover and keep water underneath simmering slowly for about 5 minutes. Lift from heat. Blend in flour, nutmeg and sugar until smooth. Slowly add the milk and stock, stirring continuously. Return top to boiler and stir sauce until it thickens. Add ½ teaspoon salt, a generous shake of pepper and the sweetbreads. Cover and cook for 2 hours over water boiling moderately (replenish if necessary). Stir in sherry and lemon juice 5 minutes before removing from heat.

Garnish with lemon slices and chopped parsley.

Serves 4.

Creamed lamb sweetbreads. Follow above recipe with these exceptions: Do not break them into smaller pieces; keep water in double boiler simmering gently. This prolonged slow cooking enriches the flavour.

Chapter 14

SOUPS

Mutton bones for stock: Shank, shaft and scrag end neck bones are best, sawn or chopped if possible. Include any other bones raw or cooked, scraps of meat and bacon rinds.

154 BASIC STOCKS

To 1 lb of bones add: 1 quart of water or stock, or vegetable water and liquor left over from canned vegetables. Include a few peppercorns, 1 large chopped onion, 1 teaspoon salt and $\frac{1}{2}$ teaspoon sugar.

Put all ingredients in saucepan. Cover, simmer $3\frac{1}{2}$ hours or longer and strain. The flavour of soups is enriched if prepared the previous day. Stocks and soups do not keep well in warm weather and must be used up quickly or boiled up every day. They will keep for some days in a refrigerator but should be covered.

Stock concentrates in the form of seasoned stock cubes, soup and stock powders provide useful instant stock. (See Glossary.)

For a basic vegetable stock of good flavour use unblemished vegetable (excluding onion) peelings, peapods, field mushroom peelings, outside leaves and coarse stalks from green vegetables, include lettuce leaves. Place in a colander under running water and wash thoroughly. Put in a saucepan and add an onion, chopped. Cover with cold water, add 1 teaspoon salt and simmer 1 hour. Strain.

155 CARAMEL SYRUP

This gives colour and added flavour to soups, stews, etc: use $1\frac{1}{2}$ cups sugar and $1\frac{1}{2}$ cups boiling water.

In a heavy-based saucepan, over low heat, stir sugar until caramelised. Remove from heat and add boiling water. Boil 5 minutes, stirring constantly. Syrup will keep indefinitely in a closed jar.

Add 2 teaspoons to each quart of stock.

156 MUTTON STOCK SOUP

To prepare soup using strained mutton stock:

Method I

1 quart mutton stock

Seasonings: add any of the following to taste:

salt or celery salt; nutmeg or mace; a bouquet of fresh herbs, bruised and tied with cotton—branches parsley, sprig of thyme, green celery tops, 1 or 2 bay leaves, or dried mixed herbs, about $\frac{1}{2}$ teaspoon.

Vegetables: about 2 cups—sliced, diced, shredded, grated or chopped.

onion	carrot
parsnip	green pepper (seeded)
tomato, peeled and chopped	turnip
celery	potato
leek with some inner green top	parsley
or 1 packet frozen mixed vegetables thawed	

Cereals: add one of the following (minimum cooking period in brackets):

1 tablespoon rice (15 minutes)	1 tablespoon sago (5 minutes)
1 tablespoon pearl barley (30 minutes)	$\frac{1}{2}$ tablespoon tapioca (45 minutes)
$\frac{1}{2}$ cup split peas (soak overnight and boil in stock until tender)	

Season stock. Add bouquet of herbs. Split peas, if they are to be included, should be added at this stage. Cover and simmer steadily about 30 minutes. Add cereal with prepared vegetables and simmer another 30 minutes or longer. Before serving add some freshly ground pepper. Remove bouquet of herbs.

To thicken: simmer soup uncovered; or mix 1 tablespoon mushroom soup powder with a little water to the hot soup, and stir in. Simmer another 5 minutes. Check seasoning.

Serve very hot with sippets and a pinch of parsley chopped.

Method II

1 quart mutton stock	$\frac{1}{2}$ teaspoon salt
2 tablespoons tomato sauce	$\frac{1}{2}$ teaspoon sugar
1 tablespoon Worcester or soya sauce	pepper—generous pinch
2 tablespoons butter	1 packet pea and ham soup powder
2 cups finely chopped or shredded vegetables—include onion and chopped parsley	

Cover and simmer stock and sauces 20 to 30 minutes. In separate saucepan heat butter until sizzling. Add vegetables, salt, sugar and pepper, reduce heat, cover and simmer very slowly for 7 minutes. Blend in soup powder and stir this mixture into stock. Simmer slowly 15 minutes or longer before serving.

157 SHEEPS HEAD SOUP

Order head in advance. It should be minus the upper jaw and halved.

1 sheeps head	1 cup split peas
branches of parsley	2 teaspoons salt
sprig of rosemary	$\frac{1}{2}$ teaspoon pepper
sprig of thyme	$\frac{1}{2}$ teaspoon sugar
2 bay leaves, or $\frac{1}{2}$ to 1 teaspoon mixed herbs	$2\frac{1}{2}$-3 quarts cold water
2 large onions	2-4 cups vegetables diced or shredded (such as carrot, celery, leek with some inner green top, peeled tomato)
bacon rinds	

Soak head in brine (2 tablespoons salt per pint of water) overnight. Wash well under cold running water. Bruise and tie fresh herbs into a bouquet garni. Knot bacon rinds. Chop onions.

Put these and other ingredients except vegetables into a large saucepan and bring to boil. Reduce heat. Cover and simmer slowly about 3 hours. Remove bouquet of herbs and bacon rinds. Add vegetables and simmer another half hour.

Remove head (see Sheep's Head Pie, recipe 97). Cool soup to allow fat to set and then lift off. If required immediately, skim off all fat. Serve with sippets (see Glossary).

158 OLGA'S ALMOND SOUP

Knuckle and bones from shoulder of
  mutton
¼ cup pearl barley
1 large onion
2 large carrots
1 small parsnip
celery tops
1 large bunch parsley
salt

pepper
milk
2 tablespoons full cream milk powder
2 tablespoons flour
nutmeg
2 oz almonds
rind of 1 orange
2 tablespoons cream

Put bones and barley in saucepan. Cover generously with cold water and bring to boil. Chop onion, carrots and parsnip. Add vegetables (the parsley and celery tied together), 2 teaspoons salt and ½ teaspoon pepper. Cover and simmer 3½ hours. Strain, and if possible leave overnight for fat to set. Lift fat off, and to each pint of stock add 1 cup of milk. Bring to boil.

To make thickening, mix milk powder, flour, ½ teaspoon each nutmeg and salt, plus a good shake of pepper, with sufficient water to a smooth paste. Stir in thickening until the soup reboils. Simmer at least 10 minutes.

Cover almonds with boiling water and leave a minute or so until skins slip off easily. Bake in a moderate oven until pale brown. Crush finely with a rolling pin and add to soup with grated orange rind and cream just before serving.

Chapter 15

SANDWICH FILLINGS AND SNACKS

General suggestions: Between slices of buttered bread or rolls put slices of cooked mutton or lamb. Season well with salt and pepper, and add one or more of the following, diced or finely chopped: capers, olives, pickled onions, gherkins, mint, chives, spring onions, celery, hard-boiled egg, chutney, minted crab-apple jelly, red currant jelly, sautéed almonds or peanuts.

Try adding a little pulped garlic and/or 1 or 2 grains of dried marjoram to the butter before spreading it.

If using either pickled mutton, mutton ham or tongue slices as filling, lightly spread with a mixture of mustard powder and cider vinegar.

159 LAMB FILLING

1½ cups lean cooked lamb finely chopped
½ cup cucumber, seeded and finely
   chopped
2 spring onions with some green top finely
   chopped or 1 tablespoon chopped chives
¼ cup grated cheese
2 hard-boiled eggs finely chopped
1 clove garlic mashed with ½ teaspoon salt

½ teaspoon celery salt
generous pinch fresh pepper
dash of red pepper sauce
pinch dried tarragon (optional)
mayonnaise, recipe 182, or french
   dressing, recipe 184
shredded lettuce leaves

Gently mix all ingredients, except shredded lettuce. (For a change fold in a little mayonnaise or french dressing.) Spread filling generously and top with lettuce. (Include a layer of sliced tomato when filling bread rolls.)

160 SAVOURY PASTE

1 lb raw lean mutton
1½ teaspoons salt
½ teaspoon sugar
¼ teaspoon pepper
1 teaspoon mustard powder
1 teaspoon ground horse-radish
½ teaspoon dried basil

good pinch marjoram
1 tablespoon cooking oil
1 tablespoon butter
1 medium onion
flour
2 rashers bacon

Cut mutton slices ¼ inch thick across the grain. Rub with mixture of seasoning and herbs. Stack in a pile.

In sizzling oil and butter sauté sliced onion until transparent. Remove and keep warm. Flour steaks and brown them.

Put onion, bacon and meat, including all the pan browning, into a bowl. Place in a saucepan containing sufficient boiling water to come half-way up the uncovered bowl. Put firm lid on saucepan and steam 2 to 2½ hours or until meat is very tender. (Replenish boiling water when necessary. Do not pour any into the bowl.) Cool and remove fat. Lift out the meat, bacon and onion and put through fine mincer. Boil the liquor rapidly to reduce it. Pound mince, adding a little reduced liquor until paste is of the required consistency.

If paste is to be kept for several weeks without refrigeration, fill jars, cover with tinfoil and tie with string. Place them in a pan with a little cold water in a cold oven. Heat oven to 300° and leave jars on stored heat until cool. Remove tinfoil and seal with a layer of hot clarified mutton fat (see Glossary) or melted wax. Store in a cool place.

161 APRICOT AND CHUTNEY FILLING

1 lb raw lean mutton or lamb
2 rashers bacon
1 medium onion
1½ teaspoons salt
generous pinch cayenne pepper
1 teaspoon curry powder
2 tablespoons flour

1 tablespoon butter
1 tablespoon cooking oil
2 teaspoons cider vinegar
½ teaspoon dried mixed herbs
1 tablespoon apple or mango chutney
1 tablespoon apricot jam
2 teaspoons soya sauce, or to taste

Put meat, bacon and onion through mincer twice. Season with salt, pepper, curry and flour, and while stirring brown in sizzling butter and oil. Add vinegar, herbs, chutney, jam and soya sauce. Firmly cover the pan and reduce heat to a gentle simmer for 1 to 1¾ hours. Remove any fat when cold.

If paste is to be stored, follow procedure in recipe 160.

162 LIVER PASTE

1 lb sheep's liver
1 teaspoon salt
pepper
2 tablespoons flour
2 rashers bacon

2 tablespoons butter
1 onion
2 tablespoons Blue Ribbon Relish, recipe 191
2 tablespoons sherry

Cut raw liver in slices ¼ inch thick. Season and coat with flour.

Cut rinds from bacon and sauté over moderate heat until fat is transparent. Remove from pan. Add butter to the pan and heat until it starts to brown. Add finely chopped onion and liver slices and sauté 4 minutes each side. After turning the slices, spread with relish. Add sherry to pan, and let it boil a few seconds.

Remove pan contents, being sure to scrape up all the pan browning.

When cold mince liver and bacon, add browning and pound to a paste.

163 QUICK EASY LIVER PASTE

To left-over liver slices add a grilled bacon rasher, the yolk of a hard-boiled egg, finely cut chives or a little grated onion. Pound to a pulp. Add a little tasty left-over gravy until paste is a spreading consistency. Check seasoning. Smear filling with mixed mustard.

164 LIVER AND MUSHROOM FILLING

1 lb liver
1 teaspoon salt
pepper
2 tablespoons butter
1 small onion
dash of soya sauce
½ teaspoon mustard

pinch of sugar
pinch of marjoram
1 packet mushroom soup powder
1 tablespoon full-cream milk powder
2 rashers bacon
1 teaspoon lemon juice

Cut liver into slices ¼ inch thick and season. Lightly brown (about 3 minutes each side) in sizzling butter with finely chopped onion. Tip into a bowl, with soya sauce, and pound to a pulp. In separate bowl mix mustard, sugar, marjoram, soup powder and milk powder. Blend in a little cold water, then stir in 3 tablespoons hot water. Put finely-chopped bacon in pan and when it changes colour blend in soup powder mixture. Stir until it boils. Add the lemon juice and stir this into the liver pulp. Put in a double boiler. Cover firmly and cook ¾ hour over simmering water.

If paste is to be stored, follow recipe 160.

165 MOUTON PATE

1 lb lean lamb, hogget or mutton
2 rashers lean bacon
1 teaspoon salt
pepper—freshly ground
½ cup cream
2 oz red wine
1 tablespoon butter

1 medium onion
1 rib celery
2 tablespoons chopped parsley
1 tablespoon green pepper
pinch of sugar
3 tablespoons breadcrumbs
2 tablespoons grated cheese

Mince meat and bacon. Season, add cream and put in electric frying pan. Cover firmly and cook at 200° from 2-3 hours. Add wine. Heat butter in saucepan until sizzling and add finely chopped onion, celery, parsley, and green pepper, with a pinch of salt, pepper and sugar. Cover firmly and reduce heat to a slow simmer for 7 minutes. Fold with bread-crumbs and cheese into the meat mixture. Simmer slowly another half hour. Use hot or cold as a filling for toasted or sautéed sandwiches, see recipe 169, or hot on croutes (see Glossary), and top with hard-boiled egg grated, a little shredded pepper green and a pinch of paprika. Use cold as a filling for sandwiches or bread rolls. Inclusion of croute topping is optional.

166 LAMBURGER SNACKS

Try these with a glass of beer or cup of coffee

1 lb lean lamb or hogget steak
1½ cloves garlic
1 teaspoon salt
1 teaspoon mustard
1 teaspoon honey
¼ teaspoon nutmeg
¼ teaspoon freshly ground pepper

pinch mixed herbs
1 medium onion
lemon juice
½ cup fine soft breadcrumbs
flour
butter
mustard or tomato sauce

Chop 1 clove garlic and pulp with salt. Mix with mustard, honey, nutmeg, pepper and herbs.

Thinly slice steaks across the grain and spread with seasoning. Dice meat and finely chop onion, or put both through mincer, using the coarse cutter. Mix in a squeeze of lemon juice and fold in the breadcrumbs.

With lightly floured hands, roll into balls and flatten a little. Sauté each side 3-4 minutes in browning butter (frying pan temperature 300-325°).

Pulp ½ clove garlic and blend with a generous amount of softened butter to spread on thick slices of bread. Place a lamburger on half the slices. Spread with mixed mustard or tomato sauce. Top with the remaining bread slices. Either serve as is ; or, as sautéed sandwiches : heat frying pan to 325°. Place lamburgers between unbuttered slices of bread. Generously butter one surface and sauté until crisp and golden. Spread with butter before turning to crisp. Serve hot.

Serves 6.

167 HUNTSMEN'S SANDWICHES

A complete picnic meal or Sunday night supper. May be prepared in advance.

Prepare Picnic Lamburger mixture, recipe 96. Leave as a mixture. Sauté in sizzling hot butter until just cooked. Put it aside until cold. (Can be stored 3 or 4 days in refrigerator).

From a square bread loaf cut slices ¼ inch thick. Spread with garlic butter, recipe 192, seasoned to taste with salt and freshly-ground pepper. On half the buttered slices spread a ¼ inch layer of meat filling. Sprinkle with a little tomato and soya sauce. Cover with sliced pickled onions or chopped chives, and finally a layer of sliced hard-boiled egg. Top with the remaining bread slices.

Stack sandwiches on a piece of plastic or waxed paper, and separate each with waxed paper. Make an airtight parcel. Top with a flat board and weight to press them evenly. Stand 2 hours or longer. Remove weight, put parcel in plastic bag and store in refrigerator. Before serving, thaw completely. Unwrap, trim crusts and cut into shapes. Arrange in crisp lettuce leaves with asparagus tips.

168 HUNTSMEN'S SAUTEED SANDWICH DIP

1 egg
½ teaspoon mustard powder
pinch salt
pinch sugar

pinch cayenne pepper
1 teaspoon Worcester or soya sauce
butter

Prepare Huntsmen's Sandwiches, recipe 167. Beat egg with other ingredients. Dip sandwiches in this mixture and sauté each side in hot butter until nicely browned and crisp. Note: Left-over sandwiches which have dried out a little may be treated in this way and make a good breakfast or luncheon dish.

169 TOASTED OR SAUTEED HUNTSMEN'S SANDWICHES

The bread should be at least 3 days old and not more than ¼ inch thick. Any of the preceding fillings are suitable.

Place either Lamburger Snack Filling, recipe 166, or Huntsmen's Sandwich Filling, recipe 167, between unbuttered bread slices. Generously spread one surface with butter and toast not too close to heat until golden brown. Turn. Spread with butter and return to the grill to brown. Serve immediately.

To sauté sandwiches, an electric frying pan heated to 325° is ideal. A heavy-based pan heated until fairly hot will suffice. As above, the filling is placed between unbuttered bread slices, and one surface spread with butter (more economical and efficient than heating butter in pan). Place buttered side down in pan. When golden brown and crisp, butter upper surface; turn and brown similarly. Serve at once, cut into shapes to suit the occasion, or keep hot on wire rack in oven pre-heated to 200°.

Chapter 16

GRAVIES, SAUCES, CHUTNEYS, GLAZES

170 GRAVY—BASIC MIXTURE

1 tablespoon flour or cornflour
½ teaspoon salt
½ teaspoon sugar

pepper—a generous shake
1 cup cold stock or water

When doubling or trebling these ingredients it is sufficient to add 1 teaspoon each of salt and sugar.

After removing a cooked roast, pour only the fat from the pan. Retain all brown bits. Add dry ingredients and a little cold water. Blend with the pan browning until smooth, and stir in stock or water. Bring to boil. Reduce heat and simmer slowly 10 to 15 minutes. Taste to check seasoning.

If meat has been marinated, add the remaining marinade with stock or water.

One tablespoon of cider, wine or malt vinegar may be added with stock or water. A dash of Angostura bitters may be stirred in before serving.

Variations: One of the following may substitute for the flour or cornflour: onion or mushroom soup or stock powder; or a soup powder plus 2 teaspoons full-cream milk powder; reduce salt.

Stir 1-2 tablespoons cream, fresh or soured, into gravy just before serving and reheat.

To substitute for stock or water: Milk may be used as stock. If insufficient browning, flavour with caramel syrup, recipe 155, omit thickening. Bring to boil and simmer slowly 2-3 minutes before serving.

Canned or fresh fruit juice (apple, peach, pear, apricot or pineapple) with cider vinegar to counteract sweetness; omit sugar from seasoning, and thicken with fresh or soured cream.

Light beer or cider and 1 teaspoon brown sugar may be used. Dilute either with apple or pineapple juice, stock or water. To thicken stir in 2 tablespoons soured cream and re-heat. For wine, see Chapter 21.

SAUCES

When preparing sauces be generous with butter. Season carefully, and taste to check. Use freshly ground pepper. Add wines, pungent herbs and spices judiciously. Too much will mar success; too little can be easily remedied. Make sure the flour or cornflour has sufficient time to cook—not less than 10 minutes.

Soup powders are seasoned so, when using them as a thickener and (or) stock substitute, reduce or omit salt.

Should the sauce or gravy be lumpy, whisk with a wine whisk or beater. This also improves the texture.

Sauce made in advance should be kept hot in a double boiler or basin over simmering water. To prevent a sauce thinning after the addition of solids, heat solids first, or sit them on top of sauce for ½ minute or so before stirring in, or else add a little at a time and keep sauce simmering.

For each cup of stock, allow 2 tablespoons butter or fat. Thin sauce for soups etc requires 1-1½ tablespoons flour per 2 pints of stock, medium sauce (to pour) needs 2 tablespoons flour etc per ½ pint stock. Thick sauce for creamed dishes needs 2 tablespoons flour etc per cup stock. Very thick sauce to coat foods or bind mixtures, e.g. croquettes, requires 3 tablespoons each of butter and flour plus 1 whole egg or yolk per 8 oz cup of stock. For creamed dishes use equal amounts sauce and solids. To bind use half sauce to one of solids.

171 WHITE FOUNDATION SAUCE

Basic Recipe

2½ tablespoons butter

2 tablespoons (rounded) flour

1 teaspoon salt

pepper—a generous shake

½ pint milk

In a heavy-based saucepan heat the butter until just starting to change colour. Draw aside and stir in the flour until smooth. Add seasoning and slowly stir in the warmed milk. Return to heat and continue to stir until sauce thickens. Reduce heat and simmer 15 minutes. If necessary transfer to double boiler.

Stock may replace the milk in part or whole. If so add 2 to 3 tablespoons cream and re-heat before serving.

172 CAPER SAUCE

Follow recipe 171. Use 5 oz stock in which the meat was poached, or a substitute and 5 oz milk. A few minutes before serving stir in a little cream. Just before taking from heat add 2 to 2½ tablespoons of capers and 2 tablespoons of the liquor.

173 COATING SAUCE

2 tablespoons butter

2 tablespoons flour

1 packet mushroom or onion soup powder

7 oz milk

2 tablespoons sherry

pinch sugar

pepper—freshly-ground

1 teaspoon lemon juice

Heat butter until it is just starting to brown, blend in the flour and soup powder. Add milk and stir slowly until mixture thickens. Add sherry gradually and stir until boiling. Reduce heat and simmer 10 minutes. Stir in sugar, pepper and lemon juice.

To serve as an accompaniment, thin with cream.

174 CURRY SAUCE

Follow recipe 171 for foundation sauce. Put in saucepan with the butter: 2 teaspoons grated onion and 3 teaspoons curry powder or to taste. Add a pinch of sugar with seasoning.

Before serving add 1 teaspoon lemon juice.

175 MUSTARD SAUCE

1 egg
1½ tablespoons sugar
1 tablespoon mustard
2 teaspoons cornflour

½ cup vinegar
½ cup stock
pepper

Beat egg, sugar, mustard and cornflour until smooth. Whisk in the vinegar and stock. Cook in double boiler or tip into a heavy-based saucepan and stir continuously until the mixture thickens. Simmer slowly 15 minutes or longer. Add freshly-ground pepper.

176 LAGER SAUCE

For a fresh or salt joint steamed or poached with vegetables.

3 tablespoons fat
3 tablespoons chopped parsley
3 tablespoons flour
1 cup lager or light beer
1½ cups liquor from meat

strained vegetables
lemon juice
pepper
salt

Heat the fat reserved from cooking liquor and when sizzling add parsley. Reduce heat and cover saucepan. Gently simmer for 5 minutes but do not brown. Blend in the flour. Slowly add beer, stirring continuously. When mixture begins to thicken add the hot liquor from joint and strained vegetables. Reduce heat and simmer at least 10 minutes. Add lemon juice, freshly ground pepper and if necessary salt to taste.

177 RED OR WHITE WINE SAUCE

1½ tablespoons butter
2 oz sliced mushrooms
¾ teaspoon salt
pinch pepper
1 tablespoon flour

2 teaspoons onion soup powder
1 cup hot water
½ cup red or white wine
¼ cup cream
pinch chopped parsley

Melt butter in saucepan, sprinkle in the flour and when starting to brown add mushrooms, salt and pepper. Stir frequently for 2 minutes, lift out mushrooms and keep hot. Whisk ¼ teaspoon soup powder with water. Draw pan from heat and blend flour, salt and pepper with butter until smooth. Slowly stir in stock and wine. Continue stirring and boil 3 minutes. Reduce heat, add mushrooms and cream and simmer slowly for 10 minutes. Check seasoning and serve separately topped with parsley.

178 VEGETABLE SAUCE

Follow recipe 179. To the parsley add vegetables finely diced of shredded, e.g. onion, carrot, celery, green pepper. Good stock may partially or totally substitute for the milk, in which case add a little cream before serving.

179 PARSLEY SAUCE SUPREME

2 tablespoons butter
3 tablespoons (heaped) chopped parsley
1 teaspoon salt
pepper—a generous shake
¼ teaspoon sugar

1½ cups milk
2½ tablespoons flour
¼ cup water
squeeze of lemon juice

Melt butter in a heavy based saucepan until sizzling. Add parsley, salt, pepper and sugar. Cover closely and simmer over very gentle heat 8-10 minutes. (It must not brown.) Add milk. Increase heat and when boiling blend in the flour and water mixed to a smooth paste. Stir until the sauce thickens. Cover and simmer very slowly ½ an hour, or longer in a double boiler. Stir in the lemon juice before serving.

180 BREAD SAUCE

To serve with stuffed joints.

1 medium onion
9 cloves
1½ cups milk
1 cup breadcrumbs

1 teaspoon salt
pepper
1 teaspoon nutmeg
knob of butter

Halve onion, stud with cloves and simmer slowly in the milk about 1 hour. Put breadcrumbs from loaf aged 3 days or older in a bowl with salt, pepper, nutmeg and butter. Twenty minutes before serving strain ¾ of the milk into crumbs. Do not stir. Cover and keep warm. The milk will be absorbed. If sauce seems too dry gently stir in the remaining hot milk before serving. Top with a little chopped parsley or breadcrumbs sautéed in sizzling butter until golden.

181 MINT SAUCE

½ cup finely chopped mint (tightly packed)
½ cup sugar

1 cup boiling water
⅔ cup (or to taste) vinegar

Put mint and sugar in a bowl and with a wooden spoon or pestle pound the mixture until it becomes a moist, dark green pulp. (This can be deep frozen.) Add 1 cup boiling water, and when cool add sufficient vinegar to produce the desired sweet-sharp flavour.
Mint sauce will keep about 3 months in a screwtop jar in a cool place.

See **PINEAPPLE JUICE SAUCE**, recipe 211.

182 MAYONNAISE

1 egg
2 tablespoons sugar
1 teaspoon mustard powder

2 tablespoons malt vinegar
butter, size of walnut

Beat egg, sugar and mustard, whisk in vinegar, add butter and cook in a double boiler until thick. Stir occasionally. Cool and add up to an equal quantity of cream. (It will keep several weeks in refrigerator.)

183 PAT'S DEVIL

Topping for 4 grilled chops or 1lb steak:

1 tablespoon mango or similar chutney
1 teaspoon french mustard, recipe 185

¼ teaspoon Worcester or soya sauce
1 drop tabasco or red pepper sauce

Mix all ingredients and spread on meat when it is almost cooked. Return to grill for a minute or so until the topping is sizzling.

184 FRENCH DRESSING

3 tablespoons salad oil
3 tablespoons cider or wine vinegar
1 teaspoon sugar

½ teaspoon mustard powder
garlic or celery salt
freshly ground paprika or pepper

Beat all ingredients several minutes using a rotary beater, or agitate vigorously in a firmly covered jar until thoroughly emulsified. Will keep for months. Agitate before using.

185 FRENCH MUSTARD

1 cup cider vinegar
1 medium onion
2 cloves garlic
1½ inches cinnamon stick
2 blades mace
8 peppercorns

6 allspice
1½ bay leaves
1 egg
2 teaspoons honey
4 tablespoons mustard powder
1 tablespoon olive oil

Chop onion and garlic. Place in saucepan with vinegar, cinnamon, mace, peppercorns, allspice and bay leaves. Bring to the boil and simmer 5 minutes. Cool and strain.
Beat egg and honey together. Mix mustard with a little of the spiced vinegar and whisk into the egg. Whisk in the remaining vinegar and cook in a double boiler. Stir constantly until mixture thickens. Cool, and whisk in the oil gradually. Will keep several months in an airtight jar in refrigerator.

JEAN'S BARBECUE SAUCE, see recipe 50.
AMERICAN BASTING SAUCE, see recipe 51.

186 RED CURRANT JELLY

red currants
water
sugar

Use currants preferably not too ripe. Remove any blemishes and place in a heavy-based saucepan. Crush fruit and add just sufficient water to prevent fruit from sticking to the bottom of the pan. Put on lid and simmer slowly until pulp is cooked, about 15 minutes. Immediately pour into a flour or muslin bag resting in a colander and leave over receptacle until juice ceases to drip.
Measure juice, bring to a rapid boil and add an equal measure of sugar. Boil rapidly until a few drops jell (220° F.) when spooned on to a cold saucer. Pour into warm small jars and seal.

187 MINT JELLY

Recommended with any sheepmeat roasts.

6lb (approximately) crab-apples   1 cup chopped mint (tightly packed)
sugar

Remove stems and wash slightly under-ripe crab-apples. Put them in a large saucepan or preserving pan. Just cover with cold water and boil steadily until quite soft.
To strain juice, sit a colander over a deep receptacle standing in a washtub. Pour juice through this. Discard pulp. Place a muslin bag in the colander resting on a saucepan and pour the juice through this.
In a separate bowl add 1 cup of sugar to the chopped mint and, with a wooden spoon, pound mixture to a moist dark green pulp.
Measure apple juice by the cupful into a large saucepan. When juice is boiling rapidly pour 1 cup on to the mint pulp.
To each cup of boiling juice add ¾ cup sugar and boil rapidly. Do this in small quantities. Watch and stir frequently as the boiling syrup will rise considerably in the pan. After 15 minutes begin to test by spooning a few drops into a cold saucer, and cool a minute or two. When mixture jells (220° F.) add the minted juice and reboil a few seconds. Draw aside. Pour into warm jars and seal at once.
Note: *The quantity of apple juice may be reduced before adding sugar by boiling rapidly.*

188 APPLE MINT SAUCE

Delicious as a relish, or topping for grilled chops and steaks.

3 lb apples   ½ pint vinegar
1 lb sugar   1 cup chopped mint (tightly packed)

Wash apples. Chop and simmer in 1 cup water until very soft. Rub through a sieve and return to saucepan. Add sugar and vinegar and boil steadily ½ hour. Add mint and boil another minute or two. Draw aside. Put in warm jars and seal at once.

189 MINT CHUTNEY

1 lb sugar   2 lb tomatoes just changing colour
2 tablespoons salt   2 cups fresh mint leaves
2 tablespoons mustard powder   1 12-oz packet raisins
3 cups vinegar   2 red chillies (seeds removed)
2 lb cooking apples   1 small can pineapple pieces (optional)
4 medium onions

Add sugar, salt and mustard to the vinegar. Cover and simmer 10 minutes. Core apples, peel onions and mince with remaining ingredients, except pineapple. Add to vinegar, stir frequently and simmer at least 3 hours. Put in warmed jars, seal and leave a fortnight before use.
Some small cubes (drained) of canned pineapple may be added after 2½ hours.

190 APPLE CHUTNEY

Good with mutton curries and cold meats.

4 lb apples—not quite ripe	2 teaspoons cayenne
2 lb sultanas	3 pints vinegar
4 large onions	1 oz cloves
3 lb sugar	1 oz whole ginger bruised
¼ lb salt	1 oz allspice

Core the apples (windfalls with blemishes removed are satisfactory). Tie cloves, ginger and allspice in muslin bag. Slice onions. Put all ingredients in a preserving pan and boil approximately 3 hours. Stir frequently. When mixture is a rich brown colour and starting to thicken, discard the bag of spices. Put into warmed jars and seal.

191 BLUE RIBBON RELISH

Quickly made. Ideal for flat dwellers.

(Either canned or home-preserved peaches or pineapple may be used as the base.)

1 clove garlic	2 tablespoons soya sauce
½ teaspoon celery salt	1 tablespoon vinegar
1 rib celery	2 teaspoons mustard powder
1 bay leaf	¼ teaspoon cayenne pepper
1 cup peach syrup	pinch of ground cloves
6 large peach halves	

Chop garlic and mash with salt. Bruise celery and bay leaf and tie with cotton. Simmer all ingredients about 10 minutes. Remove fruit and pulp it with a fork, or finely chop. Boil liquor to reduce to half its quantity. Remove celery and bay leaf. Add pulped fruit and simmer very slowly 20 to 30 minutes. Put in a warm jar with a screw top.
This relish harmonises perfectly with all mutton dishes. If used as a topping for roasts, grills or sauteed meats, apply during the last few minutes of cooking.

192 BUTTER BALLS OR HOT BUTTER DRESSING

A perfect accompaniment for grills and hot vegetables.

Soften butter to a workable consistency and season each full tablespoon to taste with salt, freshly ground pepper or cayenne and a drop or two of lemon juice. Then choose one or more of the following flavourings: parsley, mint or chives, nutmeg, horseradish, ginger, curry powder, cinnamon, basil, tarragon, chopped capers or olives, onion or garlic juice, grated lemon or orange rind, or pungent herbs such as rosemary, dill, marjoram, oreganum, lemon thyme, mace. (Bruise fresh herbs before chopping finely.)
To each tablespoon of butter add a good pinch of mild fresh herbs, a very small pinch of the dried preparations, or a minute quantity of the pungent varieties. Shape into balls.
As soon as the chops or steaks are grilled to the desired degree, spread each with a butter ball and place under the grill until sizzling, sprinkle with freshly ground pepper and serve, or simply serve sizzling hot grill topped with a garnished butter ball. To garnish, re-roll in either chopped chives, parsley, mint or chervil.
Note: For a hot butter dressing, melt butter until it is just starting to brown. Add a finely chopped mild herb of your choice in the above proportions. Reduce heat for a second or two. Pour over hot vegetables or grilled meats immediately before serving.

193 PRESERVED FRUIT GLAZE

Use on joint for a special occasion.

1 small can, or home-preserved, pineapple, peaches or apricots.

Strain syrup into a small saucepan and boil rapidly to about half quantity. Stir and watch carefully as it can quickly disappear, leaving a burnt pan. The juice will thicken, and when almost tacky, immediately draw from heat and keep warm.
The fruit may be in halves, slices, diamond shapes or rings; grated, or finely chopped.
Remove cooked joint to a fireproof plate and, with a sharp knife, cut a criss-cross diamond pattern through the upper skin. Use a brush to paint the upper surface with the syrup glaze. Arrange the fruit attractively and, if necessary, secure with toothpicks. Baste with the glaze and, if possible (see note below), place under the pre-heated grill, not too close to heat. Baste several times with the remaining syrup. Watch carefully as it must not burn. Remove from heat when the glaze is lightly browned and crisp. Place on warmed serving dish. Gently remove toothpicks.
Note: *Some stoves have a separate grilling compartment with insufficient depth to permit a joint glaze or topping to be treated in this way. If so, use top oven element or, failing this, heat the oven to 500° and immediately place the joint as near the top as possible for 3-5 minutes to thoroughly heat and very lightly brown the topping.*

194 FRESH FRUIT GLAZE

For this purpose fresh fruit should be just ripe, not over-ripe. Peel off tough or inedible skins, and slice or cut to required shapes. Generously sprinkle with sugar, and stand about 2 hours. Strain the juice and add a little more sugar and a squeeze of lemon juice. The addition of a little gin or brandy at this stage is optional. Bring syrup to the boil and proceed as for recipe 193. Use thin-skinned oranges or lemons. Cut in slices or use peeled orange segments. Boil an equal amount of their juice and sugar to use as the glaze.

195 APPLE JUICE AND MINT GLAZE

2 tablespoons chopped mint   1 cup canned apple juice
sugar   2-3 maraschino cherries

Pound equal quantities sugar and chopped mint with a wooden spoon to a dark green pulp. Boil apple-juice with ¾ of a cup of sugar (½ cup if juice is sweetened) until the syrup is reduced to about half the quantity. Add mint pulp, stir and remove saucepan from heat. While still hot, spoon over the joint. Grill as under recipe 193. Repeat the baste several times.
Serve joint decorated with maraschino cherries cut in rings.
rings. After basting the joint with apple-juice glaze, fix rings with toothpicks. Baste and proceed as above.
Serve with halved cherries in the centres of the apple rings.

196 APRICOT OR PEACH JAM TOPPING

¼ cup jam
1 tablespoon cider, white wine or gin
½ teaspoon ground ginger

pinch of cayenne pepper
a few almonds chopped or slivered

Stir and boil all ingredients, excluding the almonds. Simmer a minute or so. Generously apply to upper surface of joint. Sprinkle with blanched almonds before placing under the grill until almonds are delicately brown.

To blanch almonds: See Glossary.

Chapter 17

STUFFING

Bread will not crumble satisfactorily unless it is at least three days old.
Do not stir a breadcrumb stuffing. Combine the dry ingredients by lifting and folding gently with a fork and if possible, stand for a time to infuse. Sprinkle over the liquid or beaten egg, and with a fork gently lift to moisten the mixture. Moist breadcrumbs increase in volume during cooking, so a cavity should be lightly stuffed, not packed.

197 SAVOURY BREADCRUMBS

$1\frac{1}{2}$ cups breadcrumbs

1 small onion

$\frac{1}{2}$ clove garlic crushed (optional)

2 tablespoons parsley chopped

$\frac{1}{4}$ teaspoon nutmeg

$\frac{1}{4}$ teaspoon pepper

1 teaspoon celery salt

$\frac{1}{4}$ teaspoon dried mixed herbs

Finely chop onion and crush garlic. Lightly mix all ingredients.
To moisten for use as a stuffing, add $1\frac{1}{2}$ tablespoons of milk or a beaten egg (small). The mixture should not be wet.
The addition of a small apple, peeled and finely chopped makes an interesting change.
Savoury breadcrumbs may also be used:
1. as a breadcrumb coating or topping;
2. in combination, as in lamburgers or rissoles;
3. to thicken mince or stew.

198 RED WINE STUFFING

2 cups soft breadcrumbs

1 medium onion

1 bacon rasher

3 tablespoons chopped parsley

$\frac{1}{2}$ teaspoon mixed herbs

$\frac{1}{4}$ teaspoon ground nutmeg

$\frac{1}{4}$ teaspoon pepper

1 teaspoon salt

$\frac{1}{4}$ teaspoon sugar

2 tablespoons red wine

Finely chop onion, bacon and parsley. Lightly combine with breadcrumbs. Stir in herbs, nutmeg and seasoning. Add wine, gently lift and fold to moisten mixture.
Any of the following may replace the red wine: white wine, port, sherry, cider, beer, beaten egg, milk or soured cream.

199 GIN STUFFING

Vary recipe 198 by substituting 1 tablespoon gin mixed with 1 tablespoon pineapple or orange juice instead of red wine. This will give a fine mellow flavour.

200 CELERY STUFFING

1 cup soft breadcrumbs
⅓ small cup finely shredded celery
⅓ cup grated carrot
2 tablespoons shredded pineapple
1 small onion finely chopped
1 tablespoon chopped parsley

1 rasher minced bacon
good pinch of mixed herbs
1 teaspoon salt
¼ teaspoon paprika
1½ tablespoons pineapple juice

On a sheet of plastic lightly mix all dry ingredients. Sprinkle the pineapple juice and lift with fork to moisten the mixture thoroughly.

201 SHERRIED SWEET POTATO STUFFING

3 large sweet potatoes
1 tablespoon brown sugar
1 tablespoon melted butter
2 tablespoons sherry
salt
pepper

½ cup breadcrumbs
1 tablespoon finely chopped onion
1 tablespoon chopped parsley
pineapple (optional)
1 egg

Boil sweet potatoes and peel while hot. Whip them with brown sugar, butter and sherry. Add salt and pepper to taste. Combine breadcrumbs, onion and parsley, and gently fold into sweet potatoes. Use as a stuffing or topping, or with floured hands roll stuffing into balls. Coat with beaten egg, then extra breadcrumbs, and bake around a joint until brown and crisp. For added interest place a cube of pineapple in the centre of each ball.

202 ORANGE STUFFING

1 tablespoon chopped mint
2 teaspoons sugar
1 teaspoon grated orange rind
2 tablespoons orange juice

2 cups soft breadcrumbs
good pinch pepper
good pinch marjoram
1 medium onion

Pound mint, sugar and rind to a pulp and add orange juice. Mix breadcrumbs, seasoning and chopped onion and lightly stir in the minted juice.

203 APPLE STUFFING

3 apples
2 tablespoons chopped parsley
1 tablespoon chopped onion
1 tablespoon shredded celery
2 teaspoons sugar
½ teaspoon salt

pinch chilli powder or cayenne
2 teaspoons lemon juice
1½ cups breadcrumbs
½ teaspoon salt
¼ teaspoon mixed herbs
2 tablespoons butter, melted

Peel and chop apples. Combine apple, parsley, onion and celery. Sprinkle with sugar, salt, chilli powder and lemon juice. Cover and stand about 20 minutes. Mix and lightly fold the breadcrumbs, salt and mixed herbs into the apple mixture. Gently fold in the melted butter. For a small cavity, halve ingredients.

204 OYSTER STUFFING

For a special occasion glamorise a roast leg of spring lamb with this delicious stuffing.

9 fresh oysters or 1 small can oysters
2 teaspoons lemon juice
1 cup breadcrumbs
1 teaspoon grated onion

2 tablespoons chopped parsley
$\frac{1}{2}$ teaspoon salt
$\frac{1}{4}$ teaspoon pepper
pinch cayenne or chilli powder

Chop oysters (save 2 or 3 for the gravy) and sprinkle with lemon juice. Combine the breadcrumbs, onion, parsley and seasoning. Lightly moisten with oyster liquor. Add remaining oysters and liquor to the gravy with a little sherry or lemon juice.

205 MUSHROOM STUFFING

$\frac{1}{4}$ lb mushrooms
1 clove garlic
1 teaspoon salt
pinch pepper

pinch marjoram
2 teaspoons grated onion
1 cup breadcrumbs
2 tablespoons melted butter

Chop and mash garlic with salt, pepper and marjoram. Mix thoroughly with the onion and breadcrumbs. Stir in the mushrooms, peeled and chopped. Add melted butter and with a fork gently work into the mixture.

Chapter 18

MARINADES

A marinade is a liquid in which lamb, hogget or mutton is placed to give added flavour. In addition, the acid content of the marinade (wine, beer, cider, vinegar, tomato, a fruit juice, milk or sour milk) tenderises the meat by working on the connective tissues and partially dissolving them. Where cooking oil is indicated, use the oil of your choice. The basic rule is not to use strongly-flavoured seasonings with delicately flavoured foods. The ingredients may be combined with a wire whisk or rotary beater or in a shaker. Use a container (not metal) just large enough to take the meat.

Joints should be at room temperature.

Marinate mutton joints up to 48 hours; lamb or hogget 8-24 hours. Cover the dish and turn joint occasionally to keep it moist. For small cuts, i.e. steak, chops, riblets, etc., marinate 2 hours or longer.

Drain the marinated meat, season (adjust if necessary) and follow any suitable method of cooking. The remaining marinade may be added to the stock when preparing the gravy. It may also be brought to the boil, kept warm, and used as a baste.

206 SOYA SAUCE MARINADE

½ cup soya sauce
½ cup cold water
1 tablespoon lemon juice or vinegar
2 teaspoons honey

2 tablespoons cooking oil
1 teaspoon green ginger root, crushed
½ clove garlic crushed

Mix soya sauce with water. Add other ingredients. Beat until well mixed and the honey dissolved. Stand a few minutes to infuse before pouring over the meat.

207 VINEGAR MARINADE (I)

For mutton or hogget

½ cup cider vinegar
1 tablespoon cooking oil
1 tablespoon honey
2 cloves garlic, crushed

1 teaspoon mustard
½ teaspoon dried tarragon
3 peppercorns crushed
bouquet of mint and bay leaf

Combine all ingredients in saucepan. Warm and stir until the honey is dissolved. Whisk well and pour over cubed meat or chops, etc. Turn occasionally and marinate 1-2 hours. Drain meat and remove bouquet. Add ¼ teaspoon salt to marinade and use it as a baste. To marinate a lamb joint replace vinegar with lemon juice.

208 VINEGAR MARINADE (II)

¼ cup cider vinegar
1 tablespoon sugar
1 teaspoon mustard
¼ teaspoon dried tarragon

1 pinch cayenne pepper
8 peppercorns
1 small onion grated

Put vinegar in shaker, add other ingredients and shake to mix.

See **AMERICAN MARINADE**, recipe 51.

209 RED OR WHITE WINE MARINADE

Use red wine to marinade mutton and hogget; white wine for lamb.

½ cup red or white wine
1½ tablespoons cooking oil

1 clove garlic crushed
good pinch of cayenne

Beat vigorously or agitate ingredients. Marinate cubed mutton, liver or chops, etc., up to 12 hours; a mutton joint up to 24 hours. Allow lamb and hogget cuts 1-12 hours. Turn occasionally to keep moist. Drain and season meat before cooking.
Either boil the remaining marinade, keep it warm and use as a baste, or add it to the stock when preparing the gravy.
Note: If these ingredients need to be doubled to marinate a large joint, the amount of cooking oil need not be increased.

210 APPLE JUICE MARINADE

½ cup canned apple juice
¼ cup cider vinegar
1-2 tablespoons cooking oil

1 tablespoon brown sugar
¼ teaspoon ground cinnamon
¼ teaspoon cloves

Combine all ingredients well. Pour over mutton, hogget or lamb joint and marinate 8-24 hours. Turn occasionally. Season joint and use as a baste or bake joint with the marinade. Keep pan covered, and baste or turn once or twice while cooking.

211 PINEAPPLE JUICE MARINADE OR SAUCE

½ cup pineapple juice
1 clove garlic crushed with salt
1 teaspoon chopped mint
1 tablespoon lemon juice

½ teaspoon salt
½ teaspoon mustard
½ teaspoon lemon rind
pinch cayenne

Combine all ingredients well and stand to infuse. Marinate meat up to 8 hours. To serve as a sauce, boil ingredients to reduce by almost half. Add a little madeira wine to taste. Simmer and add 2 tablespoons cream. Re-heat but do not boil.

212 CITRUS MARINADE

Use for mutton, hogget or lamb

1 cup orange juice
3 tablespoons lemon juice
3 tablespoons corn oil
2 teaspoons honey

2 teaspoons mustard powder
$\frac{1}{4}$ cup chopped mint leaves
1 clove garlic well crushed
4 peppercorns, crushed

Beat all ingredients well and pour over meat. Turn frequently and marinate about 12 hours. Drain and season meat. Use marinade as a baste and add remainder to gravy.

213 TOMATO JUICE MARINADE

1 cup strained tomato juice
$\frac{1}{2}$ apple grated
$\frac{1}{2}$ clove garlic crushed
1 rib celery bruised
1 bay leaf
1 tablespoon cider vinegar

1 teaspoon Worcester sauce
2 teaspoons brown sugar
1 teaspoon dried basil
$\frac{1}{2}$ teaspoon salt
4 peppercorns crushed

Combine all ingredients well and stand to infuse. Marinate mutton, hogget or lamb 6-12 hours. Remove celery and bay leaf before adding to the sauce or gravy.

214 FRESH OR SOUR MILK MARINADE

Especially good for mutton

1 cup milk
1 small onion grated
1 bay leaf

1 branch parsley, bruised, or a few cloves
$\frac{1}{2}$ teaspoon nutmeg

Combine all ingredients. Marinate 12-24 hours. Turn occasionally to keep joint moist. For sour milk marinade add 1 tablespoon vinegar or lemon juice. Season joint and cook in either marinade. Bake in a covered dish.

215 KEBAB MARINADE

2 teaspoons honey
$\frac{1}{4}$ cup hot water
2 tablespoons soya sauce
1 tablespoon cooking oil

1 tablespoon lemon juice
pinch chilli powder
1 clove garlic, crushed

Thoroughly dissolve honey in hot water. Vigorously beat all ingredients and allow to infuse before marinating cubed or diced meat.

Chapter 19

VEGETABLES, RICE, NOODLES

For a small family several vegetables may be cooked in one steamer. Only tinfoil is required to separate them, as the steam will not cause a mingling of flavours.

When using two steamers tiered, do not pack them with vegetables, as the circulation of steam must not be hindered. The saucepan, half-filled with water, must be kept constantly boiling.

For one or two people, another method of steaming is to place a wire rack with legs in a saucepan containing approximately 1 inch of boiling water. Place vegetables, separated by tinfoil, on the rack and cover firmly. Replenish boiling water when necessary.

Before steaming, season each approximate pound of vegetables with 1 teaspoon of salt.

Cooking times for steamed fresh vegetables:

The age and size of the vegetables must be taken into account.

Root vegetables peeled, washed and cut to serving size:

Potatoes (mature) halved or small, sweet potatoes, onions, medium to small, large carrots, swedes, thinly sliced, about 30 minutes.

New potatoes, young turnips, artichokes, parsnips, aubergine, $\frac{1}{4}$ inch slices, pumpkin, marrow (young), 15 to 20 minutes.

Leeks, 1 inch lengths, celery, 1 inch lengths, aubergine cases, young sweet corn, green pepper cases, 10 to 15 minutes.

Asparagus and broad beans, 10 to 20 minutes.

Aubergine: Peel and slice, chop or dice. When cooked it may be whisked with a little cream or butter. Cases are not peeled and $\frac{1}{4}$ inch thick. Scoop out pulp. Steam until just tender. (Fill with cooked pulp and suitable additions. See recipe 218.)

Whole cauliflower: Shred the surrounding stalks. Cut through the base (a criss-cross pattern); stand upright. Sprinkle with 1 teaspoon salt and a pinch of sugar. Steam 15 to 20 minutes.

Serve onions, artichokes, marrow, leeks, celery and cauliflower topped with white foundation sauce, recipe 171.

Green vegetables: Wash well. Drain and toss to shake off surplus cold water. Immediately before required slice, shred or chop to reduce cooking time. Season with salt and a pinch of sugar. If steamer is full, turn vegetables over once or twice.

Cabbage, Spinach, Silver beet—Allow the shredded stalks 15 minutes. Add the chopped or shredded leaves for the last 3 to 5 minutes.

Celery: Thinly slice outer ribs and allow 15 to 20 minutes. Inner ribs and leaf tops in 1 inch pieces, 10 to 15 minutes.

Green peppers: Remove seeds and veins before chopping or slicing. Allow 3-4 minutes.

Brussels sprouts: First soak in cold salted water, then wash well, remove any coarse outside leaves and cut a cross in each stalk base. Steam 8-12 minutes.

As cases, cut to size, wash, etc. Steam until just tender. (They may be filled with finely chopped, steamed or buttered mixed vegetables.)

116

Green peas (garden fresh): These are best cooked in 2 inches of boiling water with several bruised mint leaves, 1 teaspoon salt and 1 teaspoon of sugar. Cover closely and boil 10 minutes. Strain, and to finish cooking put in sizzling hot butter, reduce heat, cover and simmer 5-7 minutes.

Young green beans: Put in 2 inches boiling water with 1 teaspoon salt, a pinch each of sugar and dried dill. Boil 10 minutes (longer if mature). Strain and finish cooking in sizzling hot butter (see below).

Mushrooms: Trim stalks, wipe with a damp cloth, peel field mushrooms, sauté or cook in butter. To grill—place on rack, skin up, and spread with butter. In 2-3 minutes, turn and add dab butter, pinch salt and pepper and watch carefully for another 2-3 minutes.

216 TO COOK VEGETABLES IN BUTTER

To 1$\frac{1}{2}$-2 tablespoons butter add:

a pinch dried dill for beans

$\frac{1}{2}$ teaspoon grated lemon rind for egg plant
pinch marjoram for mushrooms

1 tablespoon chopped mint for peas, new potatoes or carrots
1 tablespoon chopped parsley for most other vegetables
$\frac{1}{2}$ teaspoon salt to about 12 oz vegetables
$\frac{1}{2}$ teaspoon sugar to about 12 oz green vegetables

Heat butter until it is just starting to brown and add prepared vegetables with chopped mint or parsley etc and seasoning. Stir lightly to coat with butter. Cover firmly. Reduce to low heat and allow 3-15 minutes, depending upon the specific cooking period and thickness. Shake saucepan occasionally. When cooked sprinkle with freshly-ground pepper.

Frozen vegetables are delicious cooked this way. As the blanching and freezing process breaks down vegetable cells, they are almost cooked before they are thawed. Season and cook while frozen by either method and when thoroughly heated they are usually ready to serve. (Sweetcorn on the cob is the exception and should be thawed before steaming.)

Fresh vegetables, prepare as for steaming.

Green leafed vegetables, cauliflower or celery. Add stalks to butter about 10 to 15 minutes before the shredded leaves. Fold salt and sugar through prepared greens. Cover. Lift and fold once or twice while simmering another 3 to 5 minutes. Green peppers, slice finely and simmer in butter 2 or 4 minutes.

Slow-cooking vegetables, or those cut in serving-size pieces, should be steamed first until almost tender.

Very small new potatoes, or baby carrots, should be left whole. Add 1 tablespoon chopped mint. Season and simmer as above until tender. Shake the saucepan occasionally. Slice, dice, or shred other root vegetables, depending upon their cooking period. Include a little of the inner green top when cooking leeks.

Aubergine is sliced or diced and seasoned lightly. May also be dipped in beaten egg and sautéed in butter.

Mushrooms. In most cases slice all but the small field and button mushrooms, and simmer slowly 10-15 minutes. Add a little cream to liquor.

A mixture of vegetables, e.g. finely chopped onion, parsley, celery, aubergine, green pepper, tomato, carrot, cabbage and silver beet, etc., is delicious cooked by this method. Add slower cooking vegetables first.

To serve sauce with vegetables cooked in butter:

After the vegetables have been simmering in the butter for 5 minutes, add ½ to 1 cup of heated top milk. Simmer and stir in some seasoned thickening until the sauce boils. (Allow 1½ tablespoons of cornflour or flour, ½ teaspoon salt and some pepper per cup of milk.) Replace lid and cook over low heat at least 10 minutes before serving.

217 PRESERVED OR CANNED TOMATOES

A purée to serve as a colourful winter vegetable.

1 cup tomatoes with juice	pinch basil or tarragon
a cube of butter	1 tablespoon flour
pinch salt	chopped mint or parsley
¼ teaspoon sugar	

Melt butter, add tomatoes, salt, sugar and herb. When boiling add thickening, stir, reduce heat and simmer 10 minutes. Serve garnished with mint or parsley.
Serves 4.

To bake root vegetables in their jackets:

Recommended for sound, well-shaped, mature (not too old) potatoes, parsnips, sweet potatoes and onions.
Scrub well (wash sweet potatoes and onions) and bake on oven slide in a 375° oven. Allow vegetables of medium-size 1-1½ hours or until well cooked.
Halve vegetables lengthwise. Sprinkle with salt and pepper. Spread with a little butter and serve sprinkled with chopped parsley, or place under the heated grill for a few minutes before garnishing.

To roast vegetables:

Choose mature potatoes, parsnips, mature pumpkin, sweet potatoes, onions, tomatoes and aubergine.
Peel potatoes and parsnips. Peel (optional) pumpkin and remove seeds. Vigorously scrub sweet potatoes, under running water. Dry and cut to serving-size pieces. Peel small onions and pierce in 2 or 3 places with a fork to prevent them separating. Wash and dry tomatoes, and cut out the small core.
About 1¼ hours before the joint is cooked, arrange the slow-cooking vegetables (potatoes, sweet potatoes and onions) round the roast; baste well with the pan dripping; season with salt and pepper, and turn at half-time. Allow parsnip and pumpkin 30-45 minutes.
With tomatoes, add a pinch of sugar with the seasoning and top with a little butter. Roast about 15 minutes and do not baste or turn. With aubergine, cut into 1-inch slices —season—top with dab of butter and roast 15 minutes. Turn once during cooking.
Serve root vegetables piping hot, well browned and crisp (except tomatoes and egg-plant).
Note: Prepared vegetables may first be steamed until half-cooked. Heat butter in a shallow baking pan until sizzling hot, transfer vegetables, baste, season and roast in

a 400° oven. Turn and repeat baste once or twice until vegetables are nut-brown, crisp and tender.

An uncovered electric frying pan with thermostat at 325° is also satisfactory for this purpose.

Baked pears or quinces:

These are very good with a hogget or mutton roast. They should be firm and starting to ripen. Do not peel. Wash, halve and remove core. Place round a roasting joint. Baste and sprinkle with brown sugar. Do not turn. Bake about 1½ hours, or according to size.

RICE

Long-grained rice is preferable with meat dishes. Allow 2 oz or 4 tablespoons per serving. The amount will treble in volume when cooked.

218 BOILED RICE

1 cup rice
5 cups water
2 teaspoons salt

2 or 3 lemon slices
chopped parsley

Bring water to boil. Add rice, salt and lemon. Boil steadily for 12 minutes without covering. Tip into a colander. Remove lemon and pour 1 cup of cold water through the rice. Cover with a folded tea towel and place colander over gently boiling water until required. Garnish with chopped parsley.
Serves 5-6.

219 PAN-FRIED RICE

3 cups boiled rice
1 medium onion
2 ribs celery
salt

pepper
2 tablespoons butter
2 tablespoons cooking oil

Finely chop onion and shred celery. Lightly season and cook in hot butter and oil about 10 minutes. Add rice and gently lift and stir until it is thoroughly coated with butter and oil Sprinkle generously with freshly ground pepper and continue stirring for about 8 minutes until rice is thoroughly heated.
Serves 5-6.

220 BOILED NOODLES

8 oz noodles
3-4 teaspoons salt

2 tablespoons butter melted

Boil 3 pints or more of water in a large saucepan, add salt and noodles with one end in. water. They will coil up. Boil rapidly, uncovered, 15-20 minutes until tender. If overcooked, noodles will stick together. Strain through a colander and pour a cup of cold water through. Fold in the melted butter and keep hot. Arrange noodles to surround the meat.
Serves 4-6.

221 SAVOURY RICE PAN-FRIED

3 cups boiled rice
1 medium onion
2 ribs celery
1 clove garlic
1 teaspoon salt
2 tablespoons butter
2 tablespoons cooking oil
1 inch green ginger root
1 green pepper

1 teaspoon turmeric
stuffed olives
1 cup cooked green beans or peas
$\frac{1}{4}$ to $\frac{1}{2}$ cup raisins
toasted almonds or peanuts
$\frac{1}{2}$ teaspoon grated nutmeg
2 teaspoons soya sauce
pepper
spring onion (garnish)

Finely chop onion, shred celery and add garlic crushed with salt.
Sauté in hot butter and oil about 5 minutes. Add finely chopped ginger root and green pepper, turmeric, sliced olives and beans, chopped raisins, nuts and nutmeg. Stir well and when hot add rice. Continue stirring and taste to check seasoning. When thoroughly heated, stir in the soya sauce and sprinkle generously with freshly ground pepper. Serve after a minute or two with a garnish of shredded spring onions with some green top.
Serves 6.

222 PAN-FRIED NOODLES

8 oz noodles
1 teaspoon salt

cooking oil
fresh pepper

Boil noodles as in recipe 220. Rinse well with cold water. Shake colander to get rid of any drips.
Sauté in hot oil or drop a few noodles at a time into deep hot oil or lard at 350° until delicately brown and crisp. Sprinkle lightly with salt and freshly ground pepper before serving.
Serves 4-6.

120

Chapter 20

PASTRY

Keep all ingredients and utensils as cool as possible. Too much fat will make pastry crumble. Too much flour or liquid will make it tough, also too much mixing or handling. To assess weight of prepared pastry: add weights of ingredients and allow 1 oz for liquid. An 8 oz flour mixture rolled to $\frac{1}{8}$ inch thickness is enough for an 8 to 9 inch double crust pie, pasties, etc. Allow a little more pastry if casing is to be deep. Pastry dough should be cold (not chilled) before rolling. For the final rolling it may be placed between sheets of plastic or waxed paper. Roll $\frac{1}{4}$ inch thick for a pie crust topping. Place pastry over filled pie, allow an extra $\frac{1}{2}$ inch all round to turn under and seal. Do not stretch it. With a sharp knife or serrated scissors cut to size, make 2-4 gashes as escapes for steam, unless using a pie funnel. Moisten edges with cold water, fold under and seal. Flute round edge with thumb and forefinger.

For pasties, if cutting into rounds, use saucer as a guide. Put filling on half, leaving room to seal, fold pastry, seal moistened edges. Flute and prick in several places with a fork.

To glaze pastry, brush over with beaten egg. To bake pastry the oven must always be pre-heated. If temperature is too low the pastry will not rise and if too high it will partially rise.

Bake rough puff pastry $\frac{1}{4}$ inch thick at 475°, $\frac{1}{8}$ thick at 450° for 15 minutes then reduce temperature to suit the fillings. Bake short pastry, potato pastry and quick pie crust at 400° for 15 to 20 minutes and reduce temperature to suit the filling.

Wrap uncooked pastry before storing. It will last about a week in a refrigerator. If frozen it will keep for 3 months.

223 ROUGH PUFF PASTRY

8 oz flour
$\frac{1}{2}$ teaspoon salt
6 oz butter

iced water
1 teaspoon lemon juice

Sift flour and salt. Cut butter into small pieces ($\frac{1}{4}$ to $\frac{3}{4}$ inch squares as a guide) and use a fork to lightly mix into the flour. Add the iced water and lemon juice a little at a time, just enough to make a moderately stiff dough. Roll on a sheet of plastic or a lightly floured board into a long oblong. Fold in three and give half a turn to the left. Roll and repeat this process, folding twice more. Pastry should be $\frac{1}{4}$ inch thick.

Note: *A beaten egg yolk added to the iced water and lemon juice will enrich pastry.*

224 SHORT PASTRY

½ lb flour
½ teaspoon salt
½ teaspoon sugar
½ teaspoon baking powder
1½ oz butter

1½ oz lard or
3 oz clarified fat
1 teaspoon lemon juice
iced water

Sift flour, salt, sugar and baking powder. Add butter and lard cut into small pieces. Rub into flour until it resembles coarse meal. Lightly stir in a little of the lemon juice and iced water at a time, until of a rolling consistency. Roll on a lightly floured board to a thickness of about ⅛ inch. See also recipe 223.

225 POTATO PASTRY

2 medium-sized potatoes
½ teaspoon salt
⅓ cup flour

2 tablespoons melted butter
½ to 1 tablespoon milk

Bake potatoes in their jackets. Peel when warm, add salt and mash them. With a fork work in the flour, then butter, and lastly the milk, a few drops at a time until it resembles a soft dough. (If too moist work in a little more flour.) Wrap in waxed paper and leave in refrigerator until cold and firm. Roll between sheets of plastic to about ¼ inch thick. Use for Cornish pasties, sausage rolls or meat pie.

226 QUICK PIE CRUST

6 oz butter
3 teaspoons vinegar
pinch salt

6 oz flour
1 teaspoon baking powder

Place butter, vinegar and salt in bowl and heat until butter is starting to melt. Beat well, sift in flour and baking powder and mix to a firm dough. Let it get cold in refrigerator before rolling between sheets of plastic or waxed paper. Bake 15 to 20 minutes at 400°.

Chapter 21

HERBS AND SPICES AND COOKING WITH WINE

The art of good seasoning is to use enough to enhance the flavour of the dish—not predominate. A knowledge of herbs and spices gives variety and distinction to mutton and lamb dishes, sauces, soups, and so on. There are no hard and fast rules for the use of herbs in cooking. Their use is a matter of personal taste. Until thoroughly acquainted with the more unusual flavours and combinations one should use herbs with discretion, especially the pungent varieties.

A *bouquet garni* consists of a spray of three or more of the following varieties of herbs, bruised and tied together for easy removal: parsley, thyme, bay leaves, sometimes rosemary, celery or mint.

To dry herbs:

Properly dried herbs are at least twice as strong as fresh ones from the garden so use sparingly. The majority of plants are quite hardy and easy to grow. Cut when plants are beginning to flower, on a warm, dry morning. Tie in bundles, and each day hang in the shade in a warm draught, to dry as quickly as possible. When thoroughly dry, crumble, remove twigs, bottle and label. There should be no sign of moisture in the bottle. Dry only the seeds of mustard, fennel, coriander, chervil and cumin.

Most of the herbs mentioned below are available in this dried state from food specialists throughout the country. Seeds and ground preparations are also procurable. When combining one's own special mixture, pound the dried herbs well together and store in airtight jars ready for use. It is advisable to buy only small amounts of herbs and spices at a time as they deteriorate with keeping.

Herb vinegars:

Simple to prepare. Tarragon is the best-known herb vinegar, and is recommended for salad dressings. Use cider, wine or white vinegar, as malt vinegar has an overpowering flavour of its own.

Wash and dry a large spray of tarragon and immerse in the bottle of vinegar. Cork it and shake occasionally. After three or four weeks remove the spray. Strain and re-bottle the vinegar.

When adding the spray to the vinegar, a few cloves, peppercorns, allspice and other herbs of your choice may also be included. Prepare other herb vinegars similarly.

The following list is not complete, but contains the main spices and herbs which are associated with sheepmeat cookery and accompaniments.

Allspice: Also known as pimento or Jamaican pepper. The trees are of great beauty and charm. The berries are gathered before fully ripe and are sun-dried. The flavour is a combination of cinnamon, nutmeg and clove—hence the name. Add to stews, casseroles, ground meats, sauces and pickles. Oil of pimento may be bought from a chemist.

Anise: Pungent. Frequently used in Oriental cookery. Slight flavour of liquorice. Used in some mutton dishes, with cucumber and beet and in salads and in soups.

Basil: Versatile. Use fresh or dried. Slightly clovelike in flavour. Use wherever cloves are used. Fine with tomatoes, cooked or raw, and any mutton dishes, soups or stews. Add it dried to stuffings, or fresh in salads.

Bayleaf: From the sweet bay tree (*Laurus nobilis*). Use fresh or dried, and always in a *bouquet garni* for mutton dishes; in marinades; all kinds of stews, savoury dishes and soups. Especially good with chops cooked in milk. The dried leaf is naturally much stronger than when fresh.

Borage: Easy to grow and will self-sow. The flowers are a beautiful blue and are edible raw in salads, as are the leaves and stems. Slight cucumber flavour. Use fresh with salad vegetables. Fresh or dried in curries, casseroles, etc.

Capers: Mediterranean trailing shrub. Easy to grow from seed in frost-free areas. Flower buds are gathered and pickled. Especially good with sauces to accompany sheepmeat and fish.

Caraway: A native of Northern Europe. Biennial. Grows anywhere from seed. Pungent. An acquired taste. Good with some cheese and egg dishes, mutton stews, kidneys, liver, fried potatoes, turnips, beetroot, cabbage, baked apples and sour cream.

Cardamon: Pungent. Available whole or as powder. Very good in curries, also with liver, ground and freshly chopped sheepmeats.

Cayenne pepper: Fiery. These red chillies are seeded, dried and ground. Use sparingly. Fine in stews, savoury dishes, cheese, pickles, etc. A pinch is recommended over fried potatoes and cabbage.

Celery seed: Invaluable for stews, casseroles, soups, stuffings, gravies and especially good with fish, salads, potatoes and aspics, dressings, marinades, scrambled eggs, tomatoes, beets.
To make celery salt, finely chop some celery root into a plastic bag containing some cooking salt. Shake occasionally. After a few days put through a fine sieve and store in a jar with a good lid.

Chervil: An excellent salad herb. Slight flavour of sweet aniseed. The flavour is not prolonged, so chervil should be used immediately it is chopped. Brings out the flavour of other herbs. Combines well with tarragon, parsley and chives. Add to all sheepmeats, gravies, asparagus, carrots, new potatoes, aubergines, all salads and herb butter. Especially good with egg and cheese dishes. Easily grown from seed. Prefers a shady spot. Water in dry weather.

Chillies: There are many varieties. The seeds are bitter and should be removed. Some red chillies are very fiery. Use fresh, finely chopped or minced in hot curries, etc. Dried for chutneys, etc., or ground for chilli powder.

Chives: Belong to the onion family. Grown for the fine green leaves with delicate onion flavour. Easiest to scissor-snip after washing. Very good beaten into steamed or boiled potatoes, scrambled egg, omelettes, cream cheese, or as a garnish sprinkled over sandwich fillings, buttered new potatoes, carrots and green salads. Blend chopped chives with butter and a few drops of lemon juice, and serve with sizzling hot hogget or lamb steak or chops. Easy to grow in reasonably good soil when a clump becomes established.

Cinnamon: Bark of a tree belonging to the laurel family. Oil of cinnamon leaf is available, but inferior in flavour to the bark, which is sun-dried and curls up into tubelike lengths. This bark is also ground and sold as powder. Use sparingly. Combine with sheepmeat dishes. Try a pinch with the seasoning on steaks or chops, etc. Mix a little with butter and brown sugar or honey and rub into seasoned meat before cooking. Good in curries or with baked or sauteed pears, apples or peaches.

Cloves: The yellowed blooms are gathered and dried. Use whole or ground in pickles and sauces, to stud onions and in some marinades, soup stocks, etc.

Coriander: An annual, and a member of the parsley family. Grows in Asia and Southern Europe. The seed that forms in summer is dried and improves with keeping. Has a taste of burnt orange. Sometimes used instead of nutmeg and combines well with garlic. Particularly good with sheepmeats. Try it in curries, stews, casserole dishes or the stock pot.

Cumin seed: Egyptian origin. Same family as coriander, caraway and parsley. Grows quickly. Dried seed is good with mutton curry, casseroles, rice, fish dishes, ground meats, cabbage and cheese.

Dill: Pungent. A hardy annual from the Mediterranean. Has a natural affinity with cucumber. Use fresh or dried leaves sparingly in fish cookery and salads. Dried seeds may also be used in pickles, tomato soup, lamb stews and casseroles, and with chops, string beans, cabbage, brussel sprouts, olives, sour cream, apple sauce, baked pears.

Fennel: Sweet and pungent. Flavour of anise and dill. An acquired taste. Use the fresh leaves in salads. Particularly good in sauces and fish dishes, and when cooking apples. The roots of bitter fennel, which often grows wild on the roadside, may be cooked as celeriac, and the ripe seeds used as a dried herb.

Fenugreek: Related to the clover family. Grows in Asia. Use either ground or in seed form, in lamb or mutton stews and casseroles, curries, etc. Delicious with minced meat dishes.

Garlic: A hardy perennial bulb like an onion. The white bulb, of strong odour, breaks up into separate parts or cloves of varying sizes. It has a thin, paperlike skin, which should be removed. Has no substitute. Has an affinity with sheepmeats, but introduce it with discretion and use in combination with onion. Use a garlic crusher or pulp with seasoning, using the blade of a knife. Sliver (shred) garlic cloves and place under the skin, or along the bone of joints before roasting. First make tracks with a sharp-pointed knife. Rub meat with a cut clove before cooking, or the inside of a salad bowl, casserole dish, etc. Include in butter balls, and a very small amount in sandwich butter.

To prepare garlic salt, chop about 4-6 cloves and add to a cup of cooking salt in a dry jar or plastic bag. Shake occasionally. After about three days put through a fine sieve and store in a jar with a good lid. Garlic salt and various other preparations such as garlic cream are readily available, but the bulbs are also plentiful, inexpensive, and have excellent keeping qualities. Easy to grow and increase rapidly.

Ginger: Fresh green ginger is superior to all other forms. The root, which is easily grown in a well-drained, frostfree area, is obtainable from the greengrocer. The dried-root stock and ground powder are also used extensively. Has a hot, tangy flavour and may be added to sheepmeat stews, casseroles and curries. Combines well with allspice. Use in liver dishes, sautéed or grilled fruits—apples, pears, pineapple cooked with meat; a little in split pea soup and in marinades.

Horse-radish: A strong, pungent root. Use grated or powdered in sauces, salad dressings, herb butter, casseroles, stews, steaks, etc., of lamb, hogget and mutton. Use the tender leaves fresh in salads.

Juniper berries: These trees will grow almost anywhere. Berries take two years to blacken, and only then are ready for use. The crushed berries give an interesting and unique flavour. Use in sheepmeat stews and braises, in the stuffing for joints, and particularly in gravy, heart or kidney dishes. As a substitute, oil of juniper can be bought from a chemist but should be used sparingly.

Mace: Outer covering of the nutmeg. Use with freshly ground pepper. Especially good with all fish and shellfish dishes. Use a pinch in bread sauce, stews or casseroles.

Marjoram: Pungent. From the Mediterranean. A perennial, and not difficult to grow in a warm climate. Include a fresh sprig in a *bouquet garni*. The sun-dried or powdered form should be used sparingly. It is an excellent addition to sheepmeat grills, roasts, casseroles, stews, soups, sauces, liver and mushrooms.

Mint: Generally used when serving roast hogget or mutton. Grows freely in moist spots and window boxes, and has a spreading habit. Pound the leaves to intensify the flavour.
Finely chop the leaves when dry and use with carrots, peas, new potatoes, tomatoes, orange or pea salads, tomato or pea soup; in mint sauce or jelly; marinade for mutton or lamb; aspic for sheepmeat moulds.

Mustard: Of the cabbage family. Seeds of the three plants—charlock, black and white mustard—are very hot and are ground for the condiment. Use young leaves in salad. Mustard powder is versatile; use in seasonings, sauces, salad dressings and pickles. Mix with either water, cider vinegar or white wine as an accompanying condiment. French mustard is a mixture of mustard, vinegar, olive oil, herbs, seasoning and egg (see recipe 185).

Nutmeg: The nut that remains after removing the covering known as mace. Add it freshly grated to mashed potatoes, spinach, cauliflower, bread sauce, stews, casseroles, stuffings and all fish and cheese dishes.

Nasturtium: The half-ripened seed is added to mustard pickle and, as a substitute for capers, it is pickled when young, fresh and green. The young leaves and flowers are attractive in salads.

Oreganum: A wild type of marjoram, use similarly.

Paprika: From the same plant as cayenne, and less peppery and may be used as a substitute. (Chilli is the Mexican name for all varieties of capsicum plants. There are literally hundreds of varieties.) Their consumption is enormous in tropical countries. Sweet and spicy. Use lavishly and at will. Good with any sheepmeat dishes, potatoes egg and cheese dishes. Hungarian paprika is recommended. Buy in small quantities, as it deteriorates with keeping.

Parsley: The stalks and root have more flavour than the leaves. All three can be used generously in a *bouquet garni*, egg, cheese, and fish dishes, salads, sauces, ground meats and stuffings. Use the vivid green and curly leaves to garnish. Fresh seed should be sown annually. It should be grown in every garden, or in a tall pot to accommodate the long tap root. Likes good soil and reasonable moisture. Freshly gathered parsley contains an appreciable amount of vitamin C.

Peppercorns: Dried berries of the pepper plant. Black pepper is ground from the whole peppercorn. Freshly ground, it will add to the flavour of many dishes. Use generously when cooking and before serving all savoury and meat dishes, casseroles, grills and so on. White pepper is more pungent and comes from the inner portion of the berry.

Rosemary: Pungent, native of the Mediterranean. Versatile, but the fresh or dried leaves should be used sparingly. Good with sheepmeats. Place a spray under a leg of lamb in the roasting dish, or nick the skin in several places and insert a bruised leaf. Use in stuffings or soups, marinades, and in a *bouquet garni*. Fry a little in scrambled eggs and omelettes. Evergreen and easy to grow from a cutting.

Sage: Easy to grow from a cutting. Use sparingly in stuffings, stews, soups, liver pâté, ground meats, gravies, and with onions, tomatoes and carrots.

Saffron: A yellow powder from the dried pistils of the crocus-like flowers. Can be bought in block form from a chemist, or as a powder from a food specialist. Use in saffron butter, with lamb dishes, rice or curry; also in cakes. A pinch improves the flavour of many sauces.

Savory: Mediterranean. Summer savory is an annual. Strongly aromatic, it has an affinity with broad beans, and the finely chopped fresh leaves should also be tried with green peas and melted butter. Can be used in the *bouquet garni*. Winter savory is a perennial and evergreen. Use the dried herb with liver, stews, casseroles, etc.

Sesame seeds: Add to a topping for savoury dishes and casseroles. Good with potatoes or noodles, cutlets, grills, etc.

Tarragon: An important and versatile herb. Strongly flavoured, and similar to chervil. Use the leaves fresh in a *bouquet garni* or, during winter, in their dried state with sheep-meats, tongues, fish, chicken, potatoes, mushrooms, stuffings, marinades, mustard and herb sauces and butter balls. Perennial, and will grow from a cutting in a sunny, well-drained spot. The leaves may be blanched and deep frozen.

Thyme: Pungent—a very useful herb. Use a sprig with a bay leaf and branch of parsley in a *bouquet garni*. Add sparingly to casseroles, stews, ground meats, soups, stocks, tomato dishes, fish, cheese, eggs, aspics, stuffings, carrots, onions, potatoes and peas. Cuttings grow easily in poor soil or in a pot or window box.

Turmeric (or Indian saffron): Dried root stock closely related to ginger. Its culinary uses are chiefly in curry powder and pickles. It may also be used sparingly in rice and savoury dishes.

Watercress: Delicious in salads, sandwiches, soups and as a garnish. Grows freely —usually in running water. It may also be grown in a deeply dug and moist trench. If gathered from water to which animals have access rinse in mild solution of potassium permanganate, and then in cold tap water before use.

COOKING WITH WINE, BEER, CIDER AND GIN

Wine enhances the flavour of sheepmeats and also acts as a tenderiser. It is as simple to use as vanilla or lemon juice. For hogget or mutton dishes use preferably a dry red wine, port or sherry. For spring lamb a dry white wine, i.e. sauterne or chablis. Add wine sparingly. Its purpose is to refine, not predominate in the flavour of the dish. The alcohol will evaporate during the cooking process. If adding wine to a preparation just before serving, boil it for a few seconds to dissipate the alcohol.

The more pungent herbs should be omitted and the usual seasonings included.

In the case of a wine marinade, or a joint cooked with wine, the container should, if possible, be just large enough to hold the joint and, when necessary, have a firm lid.

Beer (may be diluted if desired) is a nutritious and delicious stock in part or whole for hogget or mutton dishes requiring a long slow cooking period. A good light ale is best; bitter beer is not suitable. The following flavours combine well with beer: brown sugar, mustard, celery salt, lemon juice and rind, bay leaves, garlic, sour cream and apples.

Cider is a fine stock when preparing lamb, hogget or mutton dishes. Include the usual seasoning. Compatible additions: onion, celery, mint, cloves, tomato, green peppers, lemon juice and rind, mustard, chilli powder, apples and cream.

Gin should be added sparingly to stuffing, gravy, stews, casseroles. When a short cooking period is indicated boil rapidly for a minute or two, otherwise subject to long slow cooking. This gives an interesting flavour. In Japanese cooking use gin as a substitute for rice wine.

GLOSSARY

Aspic

A jelly made from meat stock which has been sufficiently reduced by boiling to set firmly when cold. Gelatine may be added to the strained stock, fruit, or tomato juice, etc. Aspic should be served at room temperature.

Bacon rinds

The removal of rinds before cooking is now an accepted procedure. Save these to add to stocks and knot them together to simplify removal. Or arrange over a joint when it is almost cooked and place under a heated grill until crisp and bubbly.

Bake

To cook or roast, generally in an oven, by dry heat.

Barbecue

To cook by direct heat. Meat is placed on a rack or gridiron over hot embers, usually in the open air. In an electric or gas oven the heat is generally from above the meat, and the usual term is to grill.

Baste

To moisten meat with a liquor before and at intervals during cooking. Spoon it over, or paint with a basting brush. A specially prepared marinade or sauce, or wine, beer, cider or stock are suitable bastes. Also melted butter, pan drippings or hot oil.

Blanche

To immerse nuts or fruit in boiling water for 2 or 3 minutes until thoroughly heated. This simplifies the removal of skins, i.e. shelled almonds, tomatoes. All vegetables should be blanched before freezing.

Blend

To combine gently two or more ingredients until well mixed and smooth, when a liquid is included.

Boil

To cook in liquid when the bubbles are bursting to the surface. See also to *Simmer*.

Bone

To remove the bone or bones from meat.

Bouquet garni or bouquet of herbs

A bunch of herbs used for flavouring, usually consisting of branches of parsley (stalks alone are good), a sprig of thyme and a bay leaf. Include other flavours at will, e.g. parsley root, a rib of celery or some root, sprigs of mint, a sprig of rosemary, etc. Tie with thread and bruise to intensify flavour. Immerse in stock or water for poaching, soups or stews. Remove before serving.

Braise

To brown meat on all sides in shallow, hot cooking oil, butter or fat before adding liquid. Then cook slowly with or without vegetables in a covered vessel in the oven or on top of the stove.

Breadcrumbs

For soft breadcrumbs use bread about three days old. Remove crusts, and finely crumble for stuffing, topping, coating (coarse crumbs will not adhere) and as a thickener. For baked breadcrumbs, slices of bread (not fresh) are slowly baked in the oven until they start to change colour and are crisp. Either crush with a rolling pin, or tie a bag to the mincer and grind crumbs into this. Crumbled weetbix, cream crackers, fine potato crisps, or cornflakes are also suitable as crumb coatings.

Broil

To bake using dry heat or by direct heat. In America "to broil" replaces our term "to grill".

Brown

To brown surfaces of meat or vegetables, etc, using either dry heat, or hot shallow oil or fat.

Bruise

To crush (usually fresh herbs) to intensify the flavour.

Brush

A pastry or basting brush to paint joints with bastes, glazes, etc.

Butter

As a cooking medium it imparts a delicate flavour, but will burn at a high temperature. To sauté, heat until it is just starting to brown. Add a generous amount to sauces. Melted butter heated until sizzling is the perfect accompaniment for many vegetables. Serve parsley or other herbal butter balls with grills. To butter a pie-dish or casserole, etc., smear it with softened butter before adding a mixture. Softened butter is of a spreading consistency—not melted.

Butter oil

Trade name Anhydrous Milk Fat—AMF—manufactured exclusively from cow's milk and is a high quality pure butter oil. Its only advantage over clarified butter (see below) for cooking purposes is that its purity allows it to be heated to a very high temperature without browning. Overseas, the primary use of AMF butter oil is to mix with skim-milk powder in the making of re-combined milk. See also *Ghee*.

Carve

To slice a cooked meat joint across the grain before serving, using a really sharp carving knife. Slices, which should not be very thin, will then have a fine surface. If cutting the wrong way (with the grain), the long meat fibres will be seen.

Clarify

To clear stock, melted butter, fat or oil of any suspended particles. Slowly simmer stock for about 30 minutes. Skim off any scum as it forms, then strain liquor through fine muslin. An egg-white, the shell washed and crushed, and a little finely chopped lean raw meat may be added to the cold stock before slowly heating to a simmering temperature. Remove scum and strain as above.

Butter: Melt 1 lb and simmer gently, removing any debris which rises to the surface. After about 20 minutes, it should be clear, any particles remaining on the bottom of the pan. Draw aside a minute or so before straining through fine muslin.

Mutton fat: Put 2-3 inches of malt vinegar in a saucepan and add the fat. Bring to boil and simmer slowly about 20 minutes. Pour into a bowl. When the fat is set, the debris will be in the vinegar. Lift off the pure fat, and slice off the thin layer which has been in contact with the liquid. For oil, use water instead of vinegar and treat as for mutton fat. Pour off top oil.

To clear dark fat, add a raw potato, peeled and sliced—slowly boil and when potato browns, strain.

Chop

To cut in pieces.

Coat

To cover generously with flour, beaten egg, breadcrumbs or a glaze, etc.

Core

To remove the centre from such fruits as apples, pears, etc.

Cornmeal

Ground whole-kernel corn from some of the hybrid varieties. The parent maize is ground chiefly for stock and poultry food.

Court-Bouillon

A stock (for poaching a joint) consisting of water, vinegar or wine, etc., with seasoning, herbs, spices.

Cream

To beat butter until a light creamy consistency, sometimes with honey and seasoning. Also use fresh or sour cream in sauces and to enrich and thicken gravies. See also *Soured Cream.*

Crisp

To crackle or make brittle when referring to a coating of breadcrumbs, etc. To crisp salad greens: rinse in cold water, drain, shake well and chill.

Croquettes

A mixture of raw, cooked meat and compatible ingredients finely chopped and seasoned, combined with beaten eggs or a very thick sauce, shaped, dipped in beaten egg, coated with breadcrumbs and deep fried.

Croutes or croutons

Bread shaped and fried for containing a garnish. Slice bread, preferably three days old, about $\frac{1}{2}$ inch thick. Remove crusts, cut into shapes and saute each side in sizzling hot butter until delicately brown and crisp.

Crush

Garlic, etc. Use a garlic crusher, or place the substance on a hard surface and crush with the wide blade of a knife.

Cube

To cut into $\frac{1}{2}$ to 1 inch squares.

Curdle

When an acid is added to milk it will separate or curdle. If a sauce containing egg separates, remove from heat and beat vigorously until smooth.

Cutlet

A small choice chop from the best end neck of a sheep's carcase. Also a fleshy cut of meat, usually from boned spanish neck, leg or shoulder of lamb or hogget, or a ground meat mixture in the shape of cutlets, frequently crumbed.

Dab

A small portion—usually about $\frac{1}{2}$ teaspoon.

Dash

A very small portion—usually a few drops.

Devil

To include, in a baste, marinade or sauce, a hot seasoning, i.e. chilli powder, cayenne pepper, a large quantity of mustard, red pepper or tabasco sauce, etc.

Dice

To cut into very small cubes—about $\frac{1}{4}$ inch square.

Dish

To place hot joint roast and vegetables on wire rack over fireproof dish. Stand in oven few minutes to drip before placing on hot serving plate.

Dot

To place several small bits of butter, etc., over the food surface.

Double boiler substitute

Use bowl which firmly fits saucepan. Boiling water must not contact bowl.

Dust

To sprinkle lightly with flour or cornflour, etc.

Fillet

Slices of meat with the bone removed.

Fold in

To combine ingredients lightly. Avoid stirring. Use a rubber spatula or spoon and a gentle, round sides of bowl—down, up-and-over motion. Don't hurry this procedure.

Fricassee

A stew in which the meat is not usually browned and is cooked in a white stock or sauce.

Fry

To fry in deep fat (deep fry). Fats should be clarified and without any moisture. Use a deep heavy saucepan, half full of either melted lard, vegetable fat or cooking oil. (Butter has a low heat resistance and will burn at 248°, so is unsuitable.) Heat slowly at first to required temperature, adding small quantities of food at a time (to maintain heat).

For raw foods encased in batter or egg-and-crumb coating, cook at 360-370°. For pre-cooked foods similarly encased, cook at 385°. For fillings encased in pastry (e.g. kromeskies), 390°.

Potato chips and crisps should be well dried before frying, and should fry at a temperature of 390°.

To test fat temperature without a thermometer, a 1-inch cube of bread should brown in one minute for raw fillings; in 40 seconds for cooked food, and in 30 seconds for kromeskies and chips.

Garnish

To decorate food before serving with a contrasting edible product.

Ghee

Indian name for clarified butter, made in India from buffalos' milk and in Western countries from cows' milk. As a cooking medium, ghee's value is high. When boiling, it is perfectly still and there is no spluttering. It does not burn or blacken when used for frying.

Glaze

To give a lustrous surface to joints, vegetables or fruits. Spread a heavy syrup or meat glaze on a hot joint, etc. Cold food should be glazed with aspic.

Goulash

A Hungarian term for stew.

Grate

To rub firm edible products through a grater to reduce them to small particles.

Grill

To cook foods in direct contact with high heat from below or above; also to barbecue.

Grind

To mince, or put meat, vegetables or baked bread for crumbs through a mincer, sometimes using a coarse blade.

Honey

A compatible additive to increase the succulence of sheepmeats, roasts, or grills, especially the fatty tissues.

Infuse

To allow sufficient time for flavours to mingle in liquids.

Joint

To saw through the joints of ribs and chops etc of an uncooked joint.

Kromeskies

See *Croquettes* and *Fry*.

Marinade

Usually has an acid liquid as a base with compatible additions of herbs, spices, sauces, etc. This will act as a tenderiser, improve the palatability of older animal meats and act as a pickle for a limited period if there is a high proportion of acid liquid, i.e. wine, beer, cider, vinegar, lemon juice.

Marinate

To immerse meat and let it soak in a marinade, or keep it constantly moistened for a given period.

Mask

To cover food completely with a sauce, etc.

Meat thermometer

Readily available, inexpensive and simple to use. A valuable aid in achieving a perfectly cooked roast joint.

Milk powders

Whole milk powders combine with soup powders and seasonings as a coating to sauté meats. Use less salt. Mix a packet of onion or mushroom soup powder with 4-6 tablespoons of milk powder. Dip meat first in fresh milk, then in the coating. Sauté in sizzling hot butter. As a cream substitute to add to a cooking liquor: mix about 4 tablespoons to a paste with milk. For sour cream mix with lemon juice. Work a little of the cooking liquor into this; stir it into the pan or casserole and re-heat.

Mince

To chop very finely or put through a food grinder or mincer.

Mix

Thoroughly combine and distribute ingredients evenly.

Mixer

See *Shaker*.

Monosodium glutamate

Has been in use in Eastern and European countries for centuries. A taste powder in crystalline form, it has a meaty flavour and slightly salty taste and is derived from cereal gluten. In some South American countries casein and sugar-beet products are also included in its composition.

Paper frills

Cut 2-inch strips white kitchen paper, fold lengthwise and fringe folded edge. Use as trimming.

Paste

To mix flour with a little less than half its quantity of water to a rolling consistency as a covering to seal meat if tinfoil is unavailable, or roll into small balls to protect rib ends, Crown Roast. See *Thickening*.

Pickle

To immerse in brine or vinegar solution, with or without herbs or spices, to preserve and add flavour to joints.

Pinch

This amount of a dry ingredient is as much as can be gathered between the thumb and first finger.

Poach

To cook by simmering (not boiling) a joint, or other food, in stock or water with vegetables and herbs and seasoning to taste.

Portion

Serving-size for an average-size appetite. For a large appetite increase size accordingly.

Pot-roasting

To cook a joint without first searing it or adding any liquid, in a covered dish in an oven. Steam from the joint keeps it moist.

Pound

Use a mortar, or a wooden spoon, to pound fresh herbs, etc., to a pulp. Use a meat mallet or rolling pin with vigour to tenderise meat by breaking down the tissue fibre and reducing thickness. To pulp minced meat, use a child's rolling pin with one handle sawn off.

Purée

To whisk root vegetables, boiled or steamed or cooked in their jackets, with a little hot milk or cream and melted butter until smooth and creamy. Add extra seasoning to taste. Cooked green-leafed vegetables should be very finely chopped or passed through a sieve before mixing with a little melted butter or cream and freshly ground pepper.

Ragout

A *de luxe* French stew. Usually the ingredients are not browned, and white stock is used.

Render

To separate the fat from its raw surrounding tissue. Heat it slowly. Turn at times until the fat melts and can be drained off and stored.

Roast

To bake in an uncovered shallow pan with or without fat or oil, in an oven. This cooking term is also used in the general sense, i.e. to cook, usually in an oven. When roasting in an electric frying pan, if adhering strictly to the term, the vent should be open throughout the cooking period. Is also a term used for a joint suitable for roasting, before or after it has been cooked.

Roll

Trim any rough pieces or excess fat from the boned joint. Lightly season the cut surface. If stuffing is to be included, spread it over. Roll up, starting from the lean end which should be in the centre of the rolled joint. Secure firmly with meat skewers, string, safety pins and/or sew up with a needle and thread. To roll short pastry, raw steaks, etc, place between sheets of plastic, on a cool board or firm surface, and roll with a rolling pin to the required thickness.

Sauté

(Also to pan-fry. To cook in an open pan in a small amount of hot oil, butter or fat, usually until food is lightly browned on all sides. The fat should be free of moisture and, if necessary, clarified. Heat slowly at first to evaporate moisture and prevent sputtering.

Scald

To heat liquid to a temperature just below boiling point; or, to immerse food in boiling liquid for a minute or two.

Score

To make superficial cuts in the surface of meat—usually lines, squares or a diamond pattern.

Sear

To brown meat in a hot or very hot open pan or in the oven, as a first cooking step.

Season

Herein lies the secret of sheepmeat cookery. Salt is the chief seasoning to accentuate the delectable flavour, but its presence should not be obvious. Allow 1 teaspoon per lb chopped or sectioned meat. (Joint see page 16.) Pepper, freshly ground before cooking and serving, adds piquancy. Compatible herbs and spices, lemon juice, and sauces in small or minute quantities enhance flavours and offer variety. Always taste a sauce or liquor while cooking to check the seasoning and make any necessary adjustment. Remember a pinch of sugar will improve the flavour and allay a slightly salty taste. (A raw potato, peeled and quartered or thickly sliced for easy removal and allowed to rest in simmering liquor, will also alleviate this.)

Shaker

A necessary kitchen utensil; a cylindrical aluminium container with a very firm lid, which efficiently mixes thickening in a split second. First put in cold water or stock, sprinkle in the flour, or cornflour and sometimes the seasoning. Apply lid firmly, and vigorously agitate to mix. A jar with a firm lid will also do the trick.

Shred

To cut into very thin strips.

Simmer

To cook in liquid just below boiling point, which should be continuously bubbling, but very gently.

Sippets

Cut slices of bread (not fresh) about $\frac{1}{2}$ inch, remove crusts and dice. Sauté in hot butter until evenly browned and crisp.

Skewer

A long pin of wood, metal or silver. Use when necessary to hold either the shape of a boned or rolled joint or an arrangement of food (kebabs) while cooking.

Skim

Before serving it is important to skim off all fat. When it is convenient to let a curry or stew, etc get cold, the fat is easy to lift off. If possible, in the case of a braise or stew, during the last 15 minutes or so of the cooking period tip the pan slightly, or for an oven-cooked meal, place a heat-resistant object, 1 or 2 inches high, under one corner of the vessel. The fat will then float to one spot, and be easily removed. Otherwise pour off all you can, or skim it using a deep spoon, and collect the remnants with a paper napkin, a paper hand towel, an ice cube, absorbent brown paper, or outside lettuce leaves.

134

Sliver

To cut into thin pieces about the size of matchsticks.

Soup powders

Very useful preparations available in a variety of flavours. They are seasoned—so reduce the salt a little unless using a specific recipe. May be used to replace flour or cornflour as a coating for sautéed or deep fried meats, in a savoury batter, as a thickener, or to make stock for casseroles, stews, etc.

Soured cream

The bottled cream from the milkman is pasteurised and does not sour with age. It becomes stale and eventually unfit for human consumption. To sour bottled or untreated cream, add vinegar or lemon-juice—3-4 teaspoons per cup of cream.

See *Yoghurt,* and *Milk Powder.*

Steam

To cook over constantly boiling water in a steamer with a perforated base and a firm lid. It should fit the saucepan perfectly to conserve the steam. Two steamers may be tiered on the same saucepan. The lower steamer's contents should be arranged so steam can circulate. Foods can be steamed in a closed dish or wrapped in tinfoil or cooking parchment on a perforated tray in a saucepan. The water should not, when boiling, rise to the height of the tray; therefore boil slowly. A stew or joint to be steamed may be put without liquid in an uncovered bowl in a saucepan with boiling water to reach half the bowl's height and a firm lid. To steam a liquid concoction, use a double boiler, i.e. a saucepan which fits perfectly within a second saucepan (a bowl will suffice). The boiling water in the saucepan underneath should not contact the upper container.

Stew

To cook gently in liquid for a long period—usually a mixture of meat and vegetables, cut to a suitable size, with stock and seasoning.

Stir

To blend ingredients with a wooden or metal spoon, using a circular motion. An important function is to prevent any adherence to the base of the saucepan. Use a cooking spoon, as this process will damage a good tablespoon.

Stock

The resultant liquor, usually after long, slow cooking with water and one or more of the following: bones, meat, bacon rinds, vegetables and seasoning. Stock cubes, stock powders and soup powders are readily available and offer instant stock of good quality.

Sweat

To cook meat, vegetables or fruits, usually shredded or finely chopped, just below a simmering temperature. Place food in sizzling hot butter, sprinkle very lightly with seasoning, stir to mix, cover firmly to preserve these delicious, natural aromas, and reduce heat to a low temperature. In an electric frying pan, with a correctly adjusted thermostat, sweat at 200 . On an element with degrees of heat numbered, turn to No. 1, or just below. Use one or two protective mats on an older type stove. In a double boiler the water should be simmering slowly.

Test

To test whether a joint is cooked, push a fine meat skewer into the centre of its thickest part. If the juice which escapes is slightly pink and a well cooked joint is required, return to the oven immediately for another 15-25 minutes.

Thickening

Mix flour or cornflour, seasoning, etc. with cold water or stock to a smooth pouring consistency. Sometimes used to thicken gravies, stews, sauces, etc. Stir thickening into boiling liquid, and simmer, at least 10-15 minutes to cook thickening. To mix, see *Shaker*. For other thickeners, see *Soup powders, Fresh or soured cream*.

Trivet

A small, low, perforated metal stand, used when cooking to keep a joint or other foods from the base of a roasting pan, saucepan or casserole. When roasting a joint on a trivet in an open pan in an oven with the heat from below, it will be necessary to increase the cooking period.

Thaw

To thaw frozen joints, leave unwrapped in a refrigerator for about 24 hours; chops, etc for 4-5 hours. Place packet of frozen vegetables in cold water.

Vegetable oils

Excellent cooking mediums used sparingly and sometimes in combination with butter.

Corn oil: A refined, nutritious, very light, mild-flavoured oil extracted from maize or hybrid corn.

Olive oil: An extract from olives, widely used by Europeans and Asians. Owing to its high culinary reputation in France, it rests on a pinnacle. Special uses: For cooking fish, in french dressings and mayonnaise to serve with cooked or raw vegetables. Unfortunately, extra fine olive oil is expensive and sometimes hard to obtain. Olive oil is graded and marketed according to quality. The extra fine or virgin oil is drained from the top of the vats, and is therefore lighter and purer in texture. The cheapest grade is from the bottom of the vat, and is stronger in flavour.

Peanut oil: Lighter in texture and volume than olive oil and a culinary favourite in the Near East.

Saffola: From the thistle, like a sunflower seed. Light texture. A popular edible oil because of its low calorie content.

Soya bean oil: This bean is grown extensively in China, Japan, the USA and some South American countries. It is a highly valuable source of nutriment. Also used in the manufacture of many food preparations including vegetable fat and special diet products.

Sunflower oil: From sunflower seeds. Odourless, light and nutritious. Another popular cooking oil.

Yoghurt

Cultured milk from a low fat or skim milk, reinforced with milk proteins. It is easily digested, of high diet value, and has a low calorie content. May be used instead of sour or soured cream.

INDEX

Chapter 5—Barbecues

Chapter 6—To Pan-braise or Casserole Lamb, Hogget or Mutton

Chapter 7—Minced Meat Loaves and Pies

Chapter 8—Oriental Cookery

Chapter 9—Curries

Chapter 10—Pre-Cooked Mutton Dishes

Chapter 11—Pickled Sheep Meats

Chapter 12—Mutton and Lamb in Aspic

Chapter 13—Liver, Kidneys, Hearts, Brains and Sweetbreads

Chapter 14—Soups

Chapter 15—Sandwiches, Fillings and Snacks

Page 96

Chapter 16—Gravies, Sauces, Chutneys and Glazes

Page 101

Chapter 17—Stuffings

Page 110

Chapter 18—Marinades

Page 113

Chapter 19—Vegetables, Rice, Noodles

Page 116

Many years may elapse before every household has metric kitchen scales and measures, and a stove graduated in Celsius instead of Fahrenheit. But the old familiar measures are already obsolescent, and the following conversion tables will be found increasingly useful as time goes on.

METRIC CONVERSION TABLES

Compiled by the publishers from information kindly supplied by the
School of Home Science, University of Otago, New Zealand

Metric Kitchen Measures

1 tablespoon	=	15 millilitres (15 ml)
1 dessertspoon	=	10 ml
1 teaspoon	=	5 ml
$\frac{1}{2}$ teaspoon	=	2.5 ml
$\frac{1}{4}$ teaspoon	=	1.25 ml
2 dessertspoons	=	4 teaspoons
3 teaspoons	=	1 tablespoon

Jugs and Cups

1 litre jug	=	1,000 ml
$\frac{1}{2}$ litre jug	=	500 ml
$\frac{1}{4}$ litre jug. 1 cup	=	250 ml
$\frac{1}{2}$ cup	=	125 ml
$\frac{1}{4}$ cup	=	62.5 ml
16 tablespoons	=	1 litre
4 cups	=	1 litre

Capacity

Pint	Fl. oz	Recommended measure (to nearest 5 ml)
1	20	570
$\frac{1}{2}$	10	285
$\frac{1}{4}$	5	140

Note: 1 litre (1,000 ml) = 1.76 pints.

Weight

oz	Recommended measure (to nearest 5 grams)
1	30
2	55
4	115
8	225
12	340
16	455

Note: 1 kilogram (1,000 g) = 2.2 pounds

Weights and measures of butter, flour, sugar

Butter:	2 cups	=	500 g or $\frac{1}{2}$ kilogram (kg)
	1 tablespoon	=	15 g
	1 dessertspoon	=	10 g
Flour:	4 cups (sifted)	=	$\frac{1}{2}$ kg
	2 tablespoons	=	15 g
	2 dessertspoons	=	10 g

Sugar: 2 cups $=$ $\frac{1}{2}$ kg (approx.)
        1 tablespoon $=$ 15 g (approx.)
        1 dessertspoon $=$ 10 g (approx.)

Temperature

Baking	°F	Recommended (to nearest 10°C)
Very cool	225 to 275	110 to 140
Cool	300 to 325	150 to 160
Moderate	350 to 375	180 to 190
Hot	400 to 450	200 to 230
Very Hot	475 to 500	250 to 260

Note: Boiling point 212°F $=$ 100° C; freezing point 32° F $-$ 0° C.

Length

in	cm	Recommended (to nearest cm)
1	2.54	3
2	5.08	5
3	7.62	8
6	15.24	15
7	17.8	18
8	20.32	20
9	22.86	23
12	30.48	30

Note: 1 metre (1,000 millimetres or 100 cm) $=$ 39.37 in.

1. To obtain the desired consistency for batter and dough mixtures, adjust liquid rather than dry ingredient amounts.
2. Increase or decrease in converted recipe ingredients is usually slight, so most products can be cooked in tins or other baking dishes recommended for the original recipes.
3. For simple conversions to metric quantities, replace
   (a) each oz of dry ingredients with a 25 g basic unit
   (b) each fl. oz with a 25 ml basic unit
   The quality of the product will not be affected, but basic units give slightly decreased yields.